THE SWANSEA CITY ALPHABET

HUW RICHARDS

ST DAVID'S PRESS

Cardiff

Published in Wales by St. David's Press, an imprint of
Ashley Drake Publishing Ltd
PO Box 733
Cardiff
CF14 2YX
www.st-davids-press.com

First Impression – 2009

ISBN 978-1-902719-28-3

British Library Cataloguing-in-Publication Data.
A CIP catalogue for this book is available from the British Library.

Typeset and cover design by White Lotus Infotech Private Limited, India
Printed by The Cromwell Press Group, Trowbridge

CONTENTS

In memory of my grandparents
George (1905–76) and Lily (1902–77)
Richards and to Swans fans
past, present and future.

INTRODUCTION

Some of us are born Swans fans, a few achieve it and others have it thrust upon them. With me it was a mix of numbers one and three. Supporting the Swans is a Richards family genetic defect presumed to originate with my grandfather, who moved to Swansea from Pembrokeshire in the early 1920s, but just possibly the fault of my grandmother, who came from the Sandfields and went to school at the Vetch Field Junior School, located on land subsequently occupied by a corner of the North Bank.

If simple genetics had not done the job, my father's choice of childhood entertainment was calculated to complete it, provided that Millwall at the Vetch on Easter Saturday 1966 followed by visits to Walsall, Shrewsbury, Crewe and other Midlands grounds on which the Swans played, and usually lost, did not serve as a form of aversion therapy.

It did not, so personal memories now include slightly more than half of the Swans' 82 league seasons. Not the better half, either. The period up to 1966 saw the Swans spend most of their time in the Second Division – the mood at the Vetch on that Easter Saturday was still mild bemusement at being a league lower. The seasons since, with the extraordinary just-about-worth-the-rest-of-it exception of the Toshack years, have mostly been spent in the lower two, sometimes clinging desperately even to that. The current upturn is as yet too short-lived to be taken for granted.

If I developed an appetite for stories of 'Fow, Fow, Fow, Fowler', the goals of Trevor Ford, of my father and sixth form schoolmates having rings run around them by a 13 year old who turned out to be Mel Charles and of the incomparable Ivor – whom I was just old enough to see – it was in part because these were better footballing times than my own.

You would have to be unusually unreflective not occasionally to ask yourself why you give time, money and – far more than anything else – emotional energy in unconditional support for a commercial enterprise, particularly one offering such an uncertain return on those contributions. If you love the music of Bob Dylan, the writing of P.G. Wodehouse or the plays of Shakespeare, you know they will bring you pleasure. As a football fan even the Toshack years and the club's recent renaissance have been accompanied by long periods of doubt and anxiety. Times like the re-election/relegation battles of 1975 and 2003, the near-death experience of late 1985 and the battle to oust Tony Petty in 2001–2 don't bear thinking about.

Carriers of the Swans-supporting gene at the playoff final against Barnsley. Middle row (from left) Huw Bowen, the author, John Richards, David Richards, Stan Richards.
Pic: Ron Richards (RR from here on)

So why do we care? Life is complicated and often messy. Sport is not. You know which side you are on, who you want to win or lose – and it presents you with a clear outcome. There is enjoyment and relief in a simple world in which, joining thousands of others, you can be an unconditional partisan.

It also teaches you something of life, which as my friend Brian Matthews – drawing on a lifetime following St Kilda Australian football club, which has 26 wooden spoons and more cricket legends, Shane Warne and Keith Miller, than football championships – has written is 'struggle, defeat and hope springing eternal.

The experience is no less intense at second hand. Living a 400 mile round trip from Swansea and spending numerous Saturdays reporting either rugby or cricket makes me, unavoidably, a part-time fan. There is little to match the agony of following a match through radio or text commentary, or waiting for the result to appear on a screen.

You go places – 94 different league opponents and 81 of their grounds – and meet people. You belong to a community which starts with relatives but extends to a wider circle of friends and thousands you never know, but share a cause with. Peter Stead, Huw Bowen, Peter and Bethan Charles, Len Margetson, Gareth Phillips and Martin Johnes have shared many of the matches, experiences and players who appear in this book.

An element in those friendships is shared anecdotage. Being entirely sane Eileen Bowen continues to express amused amazement that her husband and myself, mature (at least in years) men with several university degrees and a Chair in History (his) between us, can spend hours engrossed in the mix of analysis, anecdote and speculation that makes up conversation between fans of the same club.

Those shared memories and stories form this book. It is not an encyclopaedia or a history of the club. It does not claim to be authoritative or complete, but is a personal choice of names, stories and themes evoking the experience of supporting the Swans.

Some readers may feel that there is little logic in the way entries are organised, with some players listed by forename, others by surname. They are quite right. The sole reason for this is to even up, at least to some extent, the length of entries for each letter. So please do not discard this volume in disgust when Ivor Allchurch fails to appear under A or John Toshack under J. Each gets their due, just not there.

Thanks are due to Ashley Drake, who should not be judged on the basis of his choosing to live in Cardiff and, still worse, support Chelsea, for commissioning this book and bringing it to rapid fruition. Peter Charles read every entry as it was written, while Huw Bowen read the full manuscript once it was completed. Each offered pertinent criticism, his own memories and unfailing encouragement.

Particular thanks for help with the illustrations are due to Andrew Thomas and Ron Richards, both of whom provided access to their Swans photographs. Dai Smith and David Szabo also assisted with illustrations while Gavin Willacy helped with the Preston North End entry. Thanks also to John Richards, Stan Richards, Gareth Phillips, Bethan Charles, David Richards, Peter Stead, Paul Melly, Ian Lewis, Eva Melly and Mark McDonald.

This book is dedicated to the memory of my grandparents George and Lily Richards, without whom – for several reasons – none of this would be possible, and beyond that to the great mass of Swans supporters, past, present and future, wherever they may be.

HUW RICHARDS,
Walthamstow,
The day after Alan Tate's injury-time
equaliser against Watford,
August 2009.

"Is Heaven like Swansea?"
"Yes, only bigger".

(The League of Gentlemen 1999)

A is for

Alan Curtis, living proof that remembered hero-worship makes 12 year olds of us all. Like royalty, Alan must get a strange view of many people he meets, otherwise smart, articulate, worldly folk like Professors of History who admit that the encounter leaves them chuntering awestruck banalities. He is to those of us who were young in the 1970s and 1980s what Ivor Allchurch was to our fathers – the supreme Swans hero of our youth, a footballer of quality, wit and style. There is happily no need as yet to make a casting in bronze to perpetuate his memory. The original is still very much among us, genial host of pre-match hospitality at the Liberty Stadium.

That's just the latest role he has fulfilled in more than half a lifetime with the club – star player, youth coach, assistant manager and pre-match orator just the most obvious. If he is Ivor's heir as our living legend, he long ago also succeeded Harry Griffiths in an equally important role, that of faithful old retainer. It seemed inevitable he would one day become manager, a burden that he now looks to have been spared – the odd match as caretaker apart – by the club's upward mobility over the past six years.

A Rhondda boy smart enough to pass the eleven plus of unblessed memory, he also had serious genetic footballing talent as nephew of postwar hero Roy Paul. Skills evident even amid the wreckage of the early to mid 1970s – he played 37 games without scoring in the re-election season of 1974–5 – blossomed as the club revived under the management of first Harry Griffiths then John Toshack. He was capped, and scored against England, while still a Fourth Division player.

The image remains of a neat figure – there was something suitably clipped about the nickname 'Curt' – who combined extraordinary tight control with the ability to make defenders dematerialise with a drop of the shoulder and body swerve. Converted into a striker he proved peculiarly lethal in that most tense and demanding of situations – one on one with the goalkeeper – and came closer than anyone since to taking Cyril Pearce's

The hero in his playing prime

Fifty something and still looks fit enough to play. Pic: Andrew Thomas (AT from here on)

The next legend? AT

single-season scoring record with 32 goals in the Fourth Division promotion campaign of 1977–8.

He went to Leeds for a couple of seasons, and would later play for Southanpton and Cardiff, but Swansea saw him at his best. After combining with Robbie James to set up Jeremy Charles, a Swans holy trinity in operation at the perfect moment, for the goal that ensured promotion to the First in 1981, he marked the Swans' top level debut against Leeds with the goal that epitomised his skills. Taking the ball on the far right in front of the North Bank he jockeyed in towards the penalty area before a characteristic shoulder drop and side-step eliminated his marker and created space for a perfectly struck drive into the near top corner. It was the perfect exorcism of two unhappy years at Leeds and due warning of a season when Kenny Dalglish may have been a more dangerous attacker, but few others.

A brief late flourish in 1990 completed a Swans career of 364 league matches and 95 goals, only the start of a contribution that has since seen him working as Community Officer, nurturing young talent in the youth team and assistant manager under John Hollins. It was typical that on the day in 2002 when he and Hollins were sacked, he took time to donate a signed shirt for a Supporters Trust auction, and that he has since returned to assist the club in other roles.

Allen, Joe. When Dutch playmaker Ferrie Bodde went down with the injury that ended his season in November 2008, there was reason for Swans fans to be very apprehensive. While well up the Championship, a newly-promoted team might easily, deprived of its outstanding individual, end up struggling in a fiercely competitive division. That they barely missed a beat reflected the aplomb with which Joe Allen, 18 and with only seven previous league appearances, filled the vacancy. A slight figure, like fellow-midfielder Leon Britton only 5ft 6in, amid the rugged bustle of Championship midfield battles, he showed himself a composed, precise user of the ball and disciplined defender who fitted seamlessly into Roberto Martinez's tactical formations. The Swans lost only once in his first 20 league appearances. In a midfield divided between the marksmen – Bodde and Jordi Gomez – and the non-scorers, pretty much everybody else, he was definitely an abstainer with the exception of a single, highly memorable 20-yard strike that gave the Swans an 89th minute lead at Ninian Park. If Alan Curtis represents one element of Swans hinterland, the valleys, then Allen stands for another – the territories to the west. Born in Carmarthen, he grew up in Pembrokeshire. Capped by Wales during the summer of 2009, he is potentially the best midfielder produced by the Swans since Robbie James in the mid 1970s.

Ante Rajkovic was the revelation, and perhaps the outstanding on-field personality, of the greatest year in Swans history, 1981–2. Other newcomers like Bob Latchford and Dai Davies were known quantities. Ante, a tall, powerful sweeper, arrived from Sarajevo in February 1981, but injury limited his contribution to the promotion run-in, only a select audience receiving some hint of his quality in a 7–1 friendly victory over Red Star Belgrade.

Back row (left to right): Chris Marustik, Bob Latchford, Jeremy Charles, Max Thompson, Nigel Stevenson, Colin Irwin, Neil Robinson. Centre row: Phil Boersma (Assistant Manager), Alan Curtis, Ian Walsh, Dai Davies, Leighton James (now Sunderland), John Mahoney, Doug Livermore (Coach). Front row: Robbie James, Dzemal Hadziabdic, Ante Rajkovic, John Toshack (Manager), Ray Kennedy, Gary Stanley, Wyndham Evans.

Ante seated between Yugoslav compatriot Dzemal Hadziabdic and manager John Toshack in the 1982–3 team group

For most, though, he was more or less unknown when the new season kicked off. That did not last long. The Swans had had commanding central defenders before, but not one like this. He had the defensive solidity of a traditional centre-half – strong in the air and the tackle – along with footballing skills and attacking instincts that occasionally alarmed keeper Dai Davies, accustomed to more one-dimensional men in front of him, but contributed hugely to the fluid attacking patterns characteristic of that season.

Two performances epitomised his qualities. There was a hugely dominant display in the 2–0 win at Arsenal that had footballer writer Brian Glanville, never easily impressed, enthusing about his demonstration of the way a sweeper could be used to play positive football. Then at Easter came the title rivals clash with Southampton, with Ante tantalising and humiliating Saints icon Kevin Keegan several times in the opening stages by showing him the ball, taking it away and then dribbling past him. It was hair-raising, as Ante's upfield excursions often were to fans brought up on traditional British centre-halves, but a thrilling display of bravado and confidence in his own skills. Distinction of a different sort was attained captaining the team in the Welsh Cup final against Cardiff City. He committed a professional foul and became, it is reasonable to assume, the first sent-off Yugoslav ever to be handed the trophy.

Had success been more sustained, or if Swansea were not so far from London, Ante and fellow Yugoslav Dzemal 'Jimmy' Hadziabdic would have gone into the game's received history alongside the Tottenham Argentinians Ossie Ardiles and Ricky Villa and Ipswich's Dutchmen Frans Thijssen and Arnold Muhren as British football's first wave of truly top-class imports.

It didn't last. The second year was injury-hit, With an unsettled, struggling team around him Ante was not the same force, arguably outshone by fellow centre-back Dudley Lewis. He left at the end of the season, returning briefly in 1984. Nothing, though, could erase those earlier memories.

Bayo, a brick outhouse with the touch of a craftsman AT

A is also for **Adebayo Akinfenwa,** a striker of Walthamstow Nigerian origin and misleading appearance. His bulk – he was alleged to be the heaviest player in the Football League – suggested bustling physicality, but he is in fact a delicate ball-player of some skill. Perhaps the most effective foil to the peculiar talents of Lee Trundle, Bayo's misfortune is that he has gone into collective memory for his contribution to the penalty shoot-out in the 2006 play-off final against Barnsley, a stuttering run-up followed by a shot into the upper reaches of the Millennium Stadium. Now plays for Northampton, but nearly came back to the Liberty in late August 2009.

Up for the Cup in 1994. RR

And for **Autoglass,** sponsors of the cup competition for lower division clubs when the Swans won it by beating Huddersfield on penalties at Wembley in 1994. It was reclaimed, in a fresh guise as the Football League Trophy, in 2006, but otherwise subsequent Swans fortunes in the competition have been mixed. Defeat at Stevenage in late 2002, when Conference clubs were included and the Swans looked likely to be joining them the following season, looked alarmingly like the shape of things to come. Ineligibility following promotion to the Championship has occasioned only limited distress.

B is for

Brian Flynn. 'Good luck Brian, you're going to need it' was the message left by fans on Brian Flynn's car, parked outside Boston United's ground on the day of his appointment as Swans manager in September 2002. He arrived at a historic low point – bottom of the league with five points from nine games, 82 years membership in serious jeopardy. Cometh the hour, cometh the man.

An abrasive, diminutive midfielder he is perhaps the most distinguished of the locally-born outfield players who have entirely eluded the Swans. Instead he played for Burnley and Leeds, won 66 caps and appeared at the Vetch as one of the Leeds team hammered 5–1 in the Swans First Division debut in 1981.

Double Act: Brian Flynn (left) and Kevin Reeves

He returned as manager with the credentials and contacts accumulated in 12 seasons at Wrexham, winning promotion in 1993 and maintaining a higher average league position than either the Swans or Cardiff. Those contacts and his eye for a player were vital to the Swans' survival in 2002–3. Seven of the 11 players who started the last-day victory over Hull City were Flynn signings. Nor were they mere emergency stopgaps. Alan Tate, Leon Britton and Roberto Martinez, all destined for long-term importance, arrived in the space of a little over two winter months. That trio epitomised a taste for ballplayers further demonstrated the following season by the arrival of first Lee Trundle, whom he had originally taken to Wrexham from Rhyl, then Andy Robinson. As the vibrant early season promise of 2003–4, when the newly reprieved Swans won seven of their first 10 matches, scoring 24 goals, faded gratitude for his transformation of playing fortunes was overtaken by complaints about his continuing to live in North Wales and criticism of the team's fitness and lack of physicality. Yet his departure in March 2004 still seemed ungratefully premature. Since then he has nurtured a highly impressive generation of young players as manager of Wales under 21 team. His influence remains at the Liberty, both through players he signed, the renewed footballing culture he instilled while in charge and until summer 2009 the astute scouting of former assistant Kevin Reeves.

Britton, Leon's Swans career has been pursued by coincidence. Playing in the same team as solid Liverpudlian full-back Michael Howard suggested that the least Thatcherite of cities was recreating the Conservative governments of the 1980s. Later he played briefly alongside striker Leon Knight – who shared not only a forename, but a date of birth and very nearly the same height and weight. More recently his midfield partnership with Dutch playmaker Ferrie Bodde has prompted some disappointment that the Swans

Pass master at work   AT

Leon for once meets someone smaller than himself   AT

are unlikely ever to afford England full-back Wayne Bridge, preventing the completion of the Britton–Ferrie–Bridge line-up. Being mistaken for the mascot is a constant hazard.

Becoming a South Walian hero is possibly not what he had in mind as an England Youth player for whom West Ham paid Arsenal £400,000 when he was 16. His initial impact at the Vetch was extraordinary. Signed in late 2002 by Brian Flynn, whose own stature helped him recognise the dimensions of Britton's talent where others only saw his limited size, he did enough in only 25 matches for a team struggling for its life to be voted Division Three Player of the Year. Close control, speed off the mark, ability to go past opponents and immaculate passing made him lethal.

More muted under Kenny Jackett, whose taste for the physical meant that he was less sure of his place, there was a resurgence after Roberto Martinez became manager in early 2007. Perhaps the best single decision of a managership marked by tactical acuteness was Martinez's recognition that his former room-mate, whose main weakness is uncertain judgment in the final quarter, would be better suited to a more defensive role. His reward was to see Leon becoming a key element in the team that dominated League One in 2008 and won comparisons with Barcelona in 2009 as the man at the back of the midfield diamond – a composed, precise link-man and distributor who also defied assumptions about players who are both small and slight by being an effective ball-winner.

B is also for **Bartley, Danny.** Signed from Bristol City in 1972 along with centre-half Dave Bruton, Danny was a so-so winger during the grim years of the mid 1970s, transformed when Harry Griffiths took over as manager in 1975. Echoing a shift made in his own career, Harry moved him to full-back where he rapidly emerged as a highly effective performer in the modern style, solid defence supplemented by side-stepping attacking excursions up the flank and precise crosses. A small, neat figure whose build and capacity for changing direction had an echo of rugby contemporary Phil Bennett, Danny's finest moment was in one of his last matches for the Swans, at home to Chesterfield in May 1979. It was his accurately chipped cross from the left that John Toshack rose to head with rocket-like power into the Chesterfield net with eight minutes to go, breaking an hour of

Danny Bartley; moved back to take his career forward

agonising deadlock and clinching a second consecutive promotion on one of the greatest of all Vetch Field nights. Winning promotion ended his Swans career as Toshack decided he had reached his limit as a player, but he had already contributed plenty.

And for **Beynon** and two remarkable contributors to Swans success. **Benny Beynon** was arguably the club's first star, the amateur centre-forward who scored the winner in the FA Cup giant-killing of league champions Blackburn in 1914. Twice capped for Wales as a rugby union outside-half, he lost amateur status when he signed pro forms with the Swans in 1920. His departure in 1923 was similarly distinctive, as he again changed not only clubs but codes, joining Oldham Rugby League club. **Dai Beynon** was a Townhill schoolmaster of conventional classroom methods who was transformed into a coaching genius when released onto a football field. Between 1938 and 1954 he made Swansea Schools a national power, winning three English Schools championships and producing an astonishing flow of talent for the Swans. Trevor Ford credited Beynon with teaching him 'to let the ball do the work'.

C is for

Cardiff City, who represent the community 40 miles to the east once described by writer Ian Nairn as 'an unexplained malfunction between Swansea and Newport'. If the most important element in the wellbeing of any football supporter is the prosperity of their own team, a good second is a clearly-defined object of fear and loathing, a role filled with great efficiency by Cardiff. Like most really intense football rivalries, it has roots beyond the game in a wider contest between neighbouring cities of comparable size – see also Norwich v Ipswich, Southampton v Portsmouth or Liverpool v Manchester United.

Along with the visceral detestation that hangs, along with police helicopters, over derby days, is uneasy awareness that the clubs have much in common. They are currently the only Welsh teams in a league otherwise composed of

The joys of derby day   RR

90 English ones. Hundreds of Swans fans went to London in 1927 to support Cardiff City in the FA Cup final. News of Swansea's Second Division survival on the final day of the 1951–2 season was cheered at Ninian Park. The list of true Swans greats who have played for Cardiff – Ivor Allchurch, Mel Charles, Trevor Ford, Alan Curtis and Robbie James among them – almost outnumbers those who have not. Cardiff's gifts to Swansea are less numerous but include John Toshack, while Jack Fowler was born there. Alan Cork, Terry Yorath, Frank Burrows, Bill McCandless and Trevor Morris managed both clubs.

The watershed between common cause and mutual loathing may be a Welsh Cup tie at the Vetch in 1960 when Cardiff infuriated Swans fans and directors by fielding a reserve side, then annoyed them even more by winning, Cardiff directors refused an invitation to the Swansea boardroom and, including Harry Griffiths, three players were sent off. Wider tensions were created by the elevation of Cardiff to national capital in 1955 and the subsequent concentration there of government money and institutions – with the status and prosperity they bring – plus Cardiff's annexation of things cherished and previously shared, like international rugby and county cricket.

Swansea has at least retained parity on derby days – neither side has done the double and the Swans retain a marginal lead in league meetings, 18 to 16, with 16 drawn.

Some fans saw their resumption in 2008 as the main point of promotion, others as the chief drawback. The fixture also fascinates television schedulers, who ignore the fact that for most of the last quarter-century the football has been as vile as the atmosphere, and were unexpectedly rewarded by two terrific clashes, both drawn 2–2, in 2008–9. Whether either this fixation, or the parallel one expressed by many fans, is healthy is a matter for serious debate. Aside from the violence that frequently disfigures derby days, to chant 'we hate Cardiff' while playing Middlesbrough or Brighton, or have players brandishing anti-Cardiff banners at what should have been a moment of great joy, the League Trophy victory in 2006, is to take the old enemy at their own valuation, telling them how incredibly important they are.

Charles. A name to match Allchurch, rugby's Bancrofts and the boxing Curvises in the annals of Swansea sport. Perhaps the most potent Swans legend is how Leeds United 'stole' the teenage

Mel Charles prepares for action 1958

Fraternal greetings between Mel (left) and John, Swans v Leeds 1956

John Charles in 1949. There is enough truth in it for league rules to have been changed subsequently, but Leeds also recognised talent where the Swans, unusually for the period, did not. He recalled 'doing everything except play football', playing only a handful of matches in two years. Club captain Roy Paul reckoned him 'too nice a lad'. Affection and pride in his achievements were never lost, but he was no longer ours – instead much more the possession of Leeds and, above all, Turin. Juventus fans voted him their greatest foreign player, ahead of Platini.

The loss could have been greater had younger brother Mel, who went to Leeds with John, not suffered homesickness and returned to Swansea. The title of Mel's recent autobiography *In the Shadow of a Giant* says much. He was not quite as big, not quite as good – nobody was at the time – but formidable by any other standards. He was just as versatile, playing in four different positions during his 233 games for the club. It was the younger brother still playing at the Vetch, not *Il Buon Gigante* of Juventus, who was voted the best centre-half at the 1958 World Cup, while an early goal he scored against Leeds at the Vetch in the 1950s, tricking his way past big brother, was one of the few times the famously equable John was visibly annoyed. The Swans also did better from Mel's departure, with the £42,500 received from Arsenal in 1959 then the second highest fee paid by a British club.

Mel's son Jeremy carried the name into a second generation. Youngest of the holy trinity of the late 1970s, he missed the trauma of re-election and became a symbol of the rebirth nurtured by Harry Griffiths. Perhaps he did not quite fulfil the potential implicit in the family name and apparent in a

Brothers in arms. (from left) John and Mel Charles, Len and Ivor Allchurch. Northern Ireland v Wales, Belfast 1955

spectacular first season when he scored 23 goals as a 17 year old. There was, though, a passage of generations made explicit by Mel being pointed out at Swans games 'Look, there's Jeremy's dad'. Jeremy lacked his father's physical power – the same height, he was two stone lighter – and suffered niggling injuries, but had the family versatility and much of its footballing talent.

He scored vitally memorable goals – both the promotion clincher at Preston in 1981, finishing the build-up by Curtis and James – and, a mere six minutes later in playing time, the opener in the First Division debut against Leeds. As a highly saleable asset it was inevitable he would go as the club's playing fortunes and finances went into reverse, moving to first QPR then Oxford. Playing and scoring in Oxford's League Cup final victory over QPR – Robbie James was on the other side – won him a domestic British medal, something that escaped both his father and uncle.

Jeremy

Union Man; Nick Cusack

Cusack, Nick. As Nick Cusack came to the away end after his last match, at Boston in September 2002, fans pressed forward to shake his hand, slap him on the back and wish him luck. Yet he was leaving because, as manager, he had taken the Swans to the bottom of the Football League and seemed to be leading them out of it.

It was, even by Swansea standards, bizarre. Yet those plaudits and good wishes were well earned following the nightmarish period in late 2001 when the club fell into the hands of Australian-based chancer Tony Petty. Extracting the Swans from his clutches was not Cusack's achievement alone, but his presence – he was not merely club rep, but chairman of the Professional Footballers Association – ensured that every one of Petty's moves, such as his illegal sacking of seven players, was scrutinised, checked and countered. Recognition of this made him a popular hero.

He had previously been an under-appreciated player. A seasoned midfielder signed from Fulham in 1997, he was not very quick, but an excellent tackler and a reliable, if unspectacular, distributor. Those qualities were better recognised by his fellow-professionals who voted them into their Third Division select – if the least prestigious of the PFA XIs, probably the likeliest to reflect direct experience rather than reputation or media hype.

As captain his sense of responsibility extended beyond fellow-players to the fans, once leading the team to the away bank at Hartlepool to apologise for a shoddy display and a 7–1 beating.

His appointment as manager was based on the practice – when in doubt, give the job to your most intelligent current or recent player – that led later to the appointment of Roberto Martinez. It did not work. The free transfers – all the Swans could afford – he brought in neither gelled as a team nor, with the significant exception of James Thomas, functioned as individuals. The PFA, knowing a good thing when they saw one, had kept open the job offer made during the 2002 close season, and Cusack retreated with honour after nine matches, allowing Brian Flynn to begin the rescue attempt.

C is also for **Chris Coleman,** a stylish ball-playing full-back or centre-half whose services to the Swans included not only 160 league games before the age of 21, but the £275,000 received when he was sold to Crystal Palace at that age in 1991 and still more the £600,000 netted from sell-on fees when he progressed to Blackburn. An early convert to coaching following a career-ending car crash, he has emerged as a sane, lucid manager at Fulham and Coventry either side of following John Toshack's footsteps to Real Sociedad.

And for **Cyril the Swan,** a hyperactive club mascot said, incontestably, by a club director to be 'bigger than all of us' – he stands 9 ft 4 in. Cyril's activities have included abseiling from a Vetch Field floodlight, defending a Welsh FA disrepute charge, inspiring an intellectual property dispute over an advert featuring a referee harassed by a '9 ft goose' and taking part in the halftime children's penalty challenge, striking the ball better than some on-field Swans spotkicks. He has quietened somewhat following cross-breed matrimony with Sybil, from all appearances a duck, and is not to be confused with **Cyril Pearce** whose 35 league goals in 1931–2 remain a club record.

Cyril and Sybil enjoy a tender moment before the last league match at the Vetch v Shrewsbury, 2005 AT

D is for

Davies, Alan, one of the saddest figures in the club's history. He played in the FA Cup final, for Manchester United, in the fifth match of a senior career that ended at 30 with his body found in a fume-filled car on the Gower. By a grim coincidence the player he beat to the United starting line-up, Laurie Cunningham, also died young. His Old Trafford career, hampered by injury, never quite matched that initial promise, but his quality was rapidly evident when Terry Yorath brought him to the Vetch in 1987. A neat, thoughtful ballplayer, he combined particularly well with Tommy Hutchison. When both were on form, the Swans frequently benefited from the mounting exasperation of opponents trying to get the ball. Perhaps his best, and certainly his most important, match was the Third Division playoff final at Torquay in 1988. The conditions were totally against him – torrential rain, a heavy surface and rugged opposition. His precision and composure ensured midfield control, and he scored in the 3–3 draw that secured promotion. There were less happy days when the game passed him by, and these mounted in his

● SWANSEA CITY's 1987-88 Line-up . . . . BACK (from left): Joe Allon, Phil Williams, Chris Harrison, Gary Emmanuel, Keri Andrews, Alan Davies. MIDDLE (from left): Paul Raynor, David Hough, Alan Knill, Mike Hughes, Andrew Melville, Jason Ball, Ian Love, Ron Walton (Reserve-Team Manager). FRON (from left): Sean McCarthy, Terry Yorath (Manager), Dudley Lewis (Captain), Tommy Hutchison (Player/Coach), Colin Pascoe.

The ill-fated Alan Davies (back row, far right) and team-mates at the start of the 1987–8 season

second spell at the club, after following Yorath to Bradford City and back. They were typified by his last match, at West Bromwich in 1992. Taken off with the Swans two down, he saw replacement Steve Thornber – a more forceful, much less gifted midfielder who rarely scored – claim a remarkable 12 minute hat-trick to steal a 3–2 win. He was the second Swans suicide, following forward Tich Evans in the last season before Football League status was attained in 1920. Depressed by the recent death of his wife, Evans was found by club captain Jack Nicholas with his throat cut in an area underneath the main stand at the Vetch Field.

Davies, Dai. The giant cardboard hands erected by fans in the East Stand goalmouth before the Swans played Wolves in the First Division in October 1981 expressed some of the reservations about Ammanford-born goalkeeper Dai Davies, as did nicknames that included Dai the Drop and Dai Teflon. Dai, never one to be put off by what others thought, went out and recorded a clean sheet in a goalless draw. He had begun his league career at the Vetch 12 years before, deputising so well for the wacky, acrobatic Tony Millington in 1970 that he held his place when Millington recovered fitness. Rapidly sold to Everton, he returned via Wrexham in the summer of 1981 to replace the popular Dave Stewart.

Dai-version. The memoirs, translated from Welsh

Dai had the build and dentition traditional to goalkeepers – in his Wrexham days greeting a North Bank chant of 'What's it like to have no teeth?', with a huge, gummy grin. He soon found out why Swans keepers had short lifespans in this period, complaining that most of his alleged defenders were likelier to be found in the opposing penalty area than their own, but contributed his own aberrations as well as brilliantly instinctive saves. Like Leighton Phillips and Ray Kennedy he criticised John Toshack in print but differed from them by doing it in Welsh, the language in which his autobiography – later translated into English under the title *Never Say Dai* – was first published.

Board men. Chairman Huw Jenkins (left) and vice-chair Leigh Dineen. AT

Director. Current Swans chairman Huw Jenkins has been long enough in the job to know that it couldn't last. His status as local hero for astute, combative handling of the departure of Roberto Martinez and assistants in the summer of 2009 lasted precisely as long as it took the Swans to lose their first match at Leicester. The usual allegations against directors – miserliness and lack of vision or ambition – were soon voiced on the message boards.

The charge is particularly hard to make stick on Jenkins, but might be levelled at some predecessors. While economic conditions in South Wales in the 1920s would probably have stalled the Swans' upward mobility as they did Cardiff's, they were certainly helped by the Board taking nearly a year to replace Joe Bradshaw, the boss who had taken the Swans to promotion and the FA Cup semi-final, once he left for Fulham in 1926. Their successors in the 1950s allowed a sensible policy of encouraging local talent to become an ideological fetish, when investment in defenders to supplement brilliant locally-sourced attackers could have brought promotion to the First.

Swans directors have usually been local. The advantage is that they are known quantities with a commitment to club and city – brief excursions into outside ownership with Michael Thompson and Tony Petty show why this matters. The downside is that South West Wales offers only a limited supply of the very wealthy.

Typical directors have been men like Abe Freedman, chairman from 1938 to 1952, who chaired a range of local public and charitable bodies – a rare administrator respected by Trevor Ford – and his successor Philip Holden, who injected capital to avert the sale of Ivor Allchurch in 1952 and rose to became a significant Football League panjandrum, but presided over a long decline.

The tenure of Malcolm Struel might be seen as either the most successful, including the Toshack era, or the most disastrous, with spiralling costs leading inexorably to a High Court winding-up order of 1985. A glutton for punishment, Struel later joined the board of Neath Rugby Club.

Since then the longest-serving chairman has been Doug Sharpe, whose 12 years in charge were shaped by the straitened circumstances in which he found the club. Jenkins tenure has seen the Board immensely strengthened by representatives of the Swansea City Supporters Trust, first Leigh Dineen – now vice-chair – then Huw Cooze, who have given it a level of accountability and trust, no pun intended, not enjoyed by previous boards. The bottom line remains Terry Yorath's verdict on Sharpe: "Like most self-made businessmen Doug was financially driven, but I know he also had a real affection for Swansea City and he put his money where his mouth was to keep the club going."

D is also for **Dean Saunders,** victim of one of the more questionable decisions in Swans history when given a free transfer by John Bond in 1984. The striker son of former Swans full-back and assistant manager Roy, he played so well for Brighton then Oxford United that his move to Derby County made him the second Swans 'free', following Giorgio Chinaglia, later sold for more than a million pounds. He went on to cost clubs including Liverpool and Aston Villa a total of £11m in transfer fees and win 75 Wales caps. Now manager of Wrexham, he was mentioned as a possible successor to Roberto Martinez in 2009.

Dean Saunders is struck by the realisation that it all went wrong from the day he left the Vetch

E is for

Eisteddfod, National the annual Welsh-language cultural festival whose staging in Swansea allegedly presages a memorable season. The first two years following the founding of the club in which Swansea was host were 1926 and 1964, also the seasons when the Swans reached the semi-final of the FA Cup. Fifth in Division Two in 1925–6 was also the highest league placing until 1981.

The Eisteddfod returned in 1982. This time the Swans failed in the Cup, losing 4–0 to Liverpool at the Vetch, but it was otherwise the greatest year in the club's history as they occupied a top six place from the start of the First Division season, led the League as late as Easter, beat every big name except Everton and only faded in the final weeks to finish sixth behind champions Liverpool.

The 1964 semi-finalists, as yet unaware of what awaited them:
Back (from left) Eddie Thomas, Brian Hughes, Roy Evans, Noel Dwyer, Brian Purcell, Herbie Williams.
Front: Brayley Reynolds, Barrie Jones, Keith Todd, Mike Johnson (captain), Derek Draper, Brian Evans, Jimmy McLaughlin

The most recent Swansea Eisteddfod was in 2006, held at the former Velindre works rather than, as previously, in Singleton Park. This proved the best season since the Toshack era as the newly promoted Swans threatened to celebrate their first year at the Liberty Stadium with a second consecutive promotion. The Football League Trophy was claimed by beating Carlisle United at the Millennium Stadium, but most fans would happily have exchanged it for victory in the League One playoff

A rare happy ending in an Eisteddfod year.   RR

final, also at the Millennium, against Barnsley. Defeat on penalties gave further credence to an alternative theory – that Eisteddfod years end in crashing disappointment.

Europe. Not invariably popular in Swansea – West Glamorgan delivered one of the smallest 'yes' votes in the 1975 Common Market Referendum and Trevor Ford's son Martyn was a parliamentary candidate for the UK Independence Party – but Swans fans have generally liked Europe.

It has not always reciprocated. The draw for the European Cup Winners Cup, for which the Swans qualified seven times by winning the Welsh Cup, was notably mean. They were drawn in the preliminary round twice in seven excursions – the odds on this were less than one in eight – while opponents were usually from behind the Iron Curtain, with minimal glamour but far too much ability.

Most European campaigns were more day-trip than expedition, with the German Democratic Republic a particularly favoured destination. The pattern was set on debut in 1961–2, with the added complication that Britain

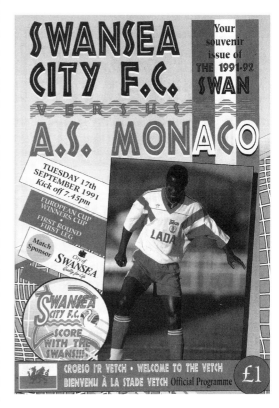

Bienvenu et Au Revoir. The last European adventure.

had yet to recognise the GDR and Motor Jena's players could not get visas. So the 'home leg' was played in Linz, Austria, 842 miles from Swansea. A 2–2 draw there was followed by a 5–1 hammering at Jena, who went on to the semi-finals.

Further East German exits were supplied by Lokomotive Leipzig in 1981–2 and Magdeburg two years later. Arriving at the Leipzig Trade Fair as a journalist in 1985 and wearing a Swans tie because it was the only one I owned, I was greeted joyously by my assigned minder, Dr Manfred Heine: "Ah, Swansea, I was their interpreter when they played here in 1981".

The only victories were in 1982–3 when Sporting Braga (Portugal) and Sliema (Malta) were eliminated before Paris St Germain administered the usual coup de grace. The 12–0 defeat of Sliema at the Vetch remains a club record, but a less vivid memory than the two later excursions. Undoubtedly the best performance was in 1990 when a team destined for 17th place in Division Three led Panathianaikos, on their way to the Greek title, on aggregate well into the second half of the second leg at the Vetch and only succumbed 6–5 to an 83rd minute winner and some questionable refereeing.

Not so close was the last appearance two years later against eventual finalists AS Monaco. The 8–0 away defeat is also a club record, with many fans fondly recalling dancing a giant conga on the away end as George Weah ran amok. The second leg saw Monaco two up before the Swans, further weakened in a period of limited local talent by a rule insisting they field seven Welsh players, realised there was no point in trying to out-football them. This was a rare occasion when a Vetch crowd acclaimed long-ball, up and under football. Monaco had never seen anything like it and the final margin was a respectable 2–1. The Football Association of Wales ensured there would be no repetition by expelling clubs who play in the English pyramid from the Welsh Cup after 1995.

Made in England. Leon Britton (left) and Darren Pratley (right) flank Dutch midfielder Ferrie Boddie AT

E is also for **England.** Large country next door, loudly proclaimed on a match-by-match basis to be 'full of ****'. Also the birthplace of, among others,

Leon Britton, Garry Monk, John Cornforth, Alan Waddle, Joe Sykes, Danny Bartley, Nick Cusack, Steve Jones, Bob Latchford, Wilfred Milne, Cyril Pearce, Sam Ricketts, Roy Saunders, Lee Trundle, Reg Weston and around 42 per cent, only slightly fewer than the Welsh, of the 750ish players fielded in the league since 1920.

And for **Evans.** If Wyndham is the best remembered of this numerous Welsh clan to have played for the Swans, he is not the only one. Small, tricky winger **Brian Evans** won selection, and played well, for Wales in 1972 when not guaranteed his place in a Swans team headed for relegation to the Fourth Division. He played 355 league games for the Swans, became the first player capped while with Hereford United, and a Swans dynast of a different sort – his son **Richie** was for years the club physiotherapist. Brian played alongside two notable namesakes, both full-backs. **Roy Evans**, a cultured defender who played in the 1964 FA Cup semi-final and twice for Wales suffered in the struggling teams of the later 1960s and was released amid a huge clearout of players in 1968. Along with centre-half Brian Purcell, another veteran of the semi-final, he anticipated Brian by joining Hereford United – then managed by John Charles and a popular destination for ex-Swans. In January 1969 they were both killed in a crash on the fogbound Heads of the Valley Road. Diametrically different in style and methods was **Micky Evans**, signed from Walsall in 1972, who also won national recognition….of a sort. In 1975 writers on *Foul*, a Private Eye-style forerunner of the fanzine movement, took note of his conspicuous contribution to the Swans spectacular disciplinary record and named him Young Clogger of the Year.

And also **Everton**, the Swans' all-time bogy club. Not only the sole team the Swans could not beat in their two First Division seasons, but the only league opponent – excluding those like Morecambe and Burton who are still to be played – never beaten at any time. That run of failure extends to 12 matches, with eight losses, and compares to a 50 per cent success record against Manchester United. Everton also played a little-remarked role in the Toshack years. Every national newspaper reader knew of the Liverpool connection, but the team at their 1981–2 peak contained more regulars who had come from Everton – keeper Dai Davies, striker Bob Latchford and two wing-backs, Gary Stanley and the red-haired vegetarian Neil Robinson.

F is for

FA Cup. If any further evidence were needed of being too used to lower division life after 24 consecutive years out of the top two leagues, it was the number of us anxiously scanning the first round draw in 2008, forgetting that this time the Swans were not involved until after Christmas.

The Swans have had glorious FA Cup moments. Beating holders Portsmouth in 2009 was latest in a line stretching back to victory over league champions Blackburn Rovers at the Vetch in 1914, the first time the Swans impinged on national consciousness. In between came the two semi-final runs of 1926 and 1964 – both including victories over Stoke City, the first inspired by Jack Fowler's goals, the second including the 2–1 quarter-final victory at Liverpool that is probably the single greatest cup day. The fifth round replay in 2009 is as far as the Swans have gone since, although fond memories remain of the 2001 Vetch replay victory over West Ham, who finished higher in the Premiership than the Swans in the Third, with midfielder Martin Thomas scoring the winner and playing most of the match with a broken leg.

But if hope springs with every cup draw, so does well-founded apprehension. Ejection by Havant and Waterlooville in early 2008 was a reminder that even the best Swans teams – this one headed for the League One title – are not immune to horrible embarrassment. Havant joined a list otherwise long on faded seaside resorts – Margate (1971), Minehead (1975) and Bognor Regis (1984) – and nondescript Midlands towns, Kettering (1974) and worst of all Nuneaton (1966 and 1993), every one guaranteed to induce a reminiscent shudder matched perhaps only by memory of the 7–0 hammering at Fulham, then a division lower, in 1995.

If the 1964 semi-final defeat by Preston remains the definitive disappointment – in 1926 eventual winners Bolton were vastly superior and rapidly three goals up – it has a rival in the quarter-final, the only other time the Swans have got so far, of 1927. It was at the Vetch, visitors Reading finished lower in the league and were poor away. But the Swans went down 3–1, so missing an all-Welsh semi-final against eventual winners Cardiff.

Fowler, Jack. Decades before 'Only one Alan Waddle' or North Bank chants of 'Lee, Lee, Lee Trundle', other heroes were celebrated in song. Jack Fowler's theme tune, 'Fow, Fow, Fow, Fowler, score a little goal for me', was the soundtrack of the Vetch in the 1920s.

He was certainly worthy of song, perhaps the greatest and certainly the most consistent goalscorer in club history, his 100 goals from 167 league matches between 1922 and 1930 the highest goals-per-game rate of anyone who has played more than 100 times for the Swans. Nor has the club had a more lethal partner-ship than his with Len Thompson, whose 86 goals in 187 games place him well up that list. In three seasons between 1924 and 1927, they scored 136 league goals. Fowler had the larger share, 75, including 28 in each of the first two seasons, a sus-tained scoring record also unequalled.

His goals drove the Swans to the FA Cup semi-final in 1926. He scored in five consecutive ties, including four against Stoke, while his five in a Third Division match against Charlton in September 1925 also remains a club record. His misfortune was scoring it in front of the smallest Vetch Field league audi-ence between 1922 and 1926, a mere 9,500 with many regulars watching the All Whites playing (and losing 39–3 to) the greatest All Black touring team a few hundred yards down the sea front at St Helen's. Rugby dominated local press coverage, but the *Daily Post* had space to report that Fowler's feat owed as much to the 'element of surprise as much as anything', implying Jason Scotland-like ability to strike fast and fiercely. Other contemporary accounts picture a player 'always willing to have a crack' and capable of shooting while running at full pace. He offered more than traditional centre-forwards as a smart ball-player noted for his skill in 'weaving'. Born in Cardiff, he started his professional career at Mardy and came to the Swans from Plymouth, then left for Clapton (now Leyton) Orient in 1930.

Fow, Fow, Fow, Fow, Fowler

He struck, though, a recurrent note in the lives of many cherished imported players – returning to Swansea after he retired. For many years he was landlord of the Rhyddings Hotel, a boxing promoter, umpire of pre-season cricket matches between the Swans and All Whites, and all-round prominent citizen.

F is also for **Frank,** which in the immediate postwar years also stood for 'physicality'. While trainer **Frank Barson's** round glasses made him look like everybody's favourite great-uncle, he was a hard man with a famous record of violence – once suspended for six months. Tackling him was, Roy Paul reported, like 'like trying to shift a steel girder'. Among his star pupils was wing-half **Frankie Burns,** sent off in the first postwar league match, a 3–2 defeat by West Brom, and frequently found helping referees with their inquiries. He could play as well and many older fans reckon his aggression, Paul's footballing skills and Reg Weston's reliability at centre-half made up the club's best ever half-back line. They also recall the Christmas 1948 brawl at the Vetch against Reading with 21 players assaulting each other in one goalmouth and Burns, generally reckoned the man most likely, the sole non-combatant. Of the same vintage was **Frankie Scrine,** grandson of an All White legend, a versatile forward famed for lethal inswinging corners. More recently came **Frank Burrows** whose staring eyes and occasionally dishevelled appearance – a Burnley-supporting friend asked 'who's that lunatic' as he waved towards Swans fans pre-match, prompting the strangled admission 'he's our manager' – and previous at Cardiff concealed a highly astute spotter of cut-price talent and deployer of scarce resources. Frank's wholly unmerited reward was the unprintable and wholly slanderous allegations sung by the North Bank choir after he returned to Cardiff for a second spell, but nobody since has matched his four and a half years (1991–5) as Swans manager and few have done more with less. **Frank Lampard,** a fairly anonymous loanee from West Ham who scored once in nine games in 1995–6, is rumoured still to be playing for one of the London clubs.

Frank Scrine

G is for

Griffiths, Harry. Look at any picture of Swans players training or relaxing in the 1950s and the eyes are drawn to one figure. A little below average height and with cherubic features, he looks ready to crack a joke or break into laughter, the natural centre of any gathering. The image does not lie. Harry Griffiths was at the centre of things at the Vetch Field for a good quarter-century, second man – and the link – in the sequence of great club servants. His youthful skills were developed by Joe Sykes, and he in turn nurtured Alan Curtis.

A member of the first postwar Swansea Schools team in 1946, he graduated to the Vetch in 1949 before National Service – a charming picture shows grinning team-mates saying goodbye to him – put his career on hold for two years. On his return he rapidly seized a first-team place as a lively, tenacious winger, making such an impression that he was capped by Wales before the

end of his first full season. The match, against Northern Ireland in Belfast in April 1953 is remembered for Wales fielding an all-Swansea forward line, Harry lining up alongside John Charles, Trevor Ford, Ivor Allchurch and Terry Medwin.

It was his only cap, but his services to the Swans were scarcely beginning.

Not least of the attributes of the gifted young players trained first by Dai Beynon with Swansea Schools, then Joe Sykes at the Vetch, were all-round skills and footballing intelligence that enabled them to master several positions. If Ivor Allchurch was the fixed point and pole star at inside-left, a galaxy of talent revolved around him. Harry moved from wing to inside-forward in 1954, more or less as Cliff Jones made the opposite switch.

In the following three seasons many good judges reckoned that the Swans, Second Division or not, had the best

Harry the manager: 'He told us to be creative, not destructive'.

forwards in the league. Two hundred and fifty-nine goals were scored in those three campaigns. Too bad the defence was not in the same class, conceding 254. Harry was an integral part of that dazzling attack, scorer of 51 goals during this period.

A further shift was yet to come in 1957 as he moved to full-back with such ease that the *Evening Post*, which had been advocating a Wales recall at inside-forward, shifted seamlessly to calling for him to be picked at full-back. He lasted there almost as long as the Swans did in Division Two, finally leaving after 424 league games and 71 goals to take over as manager at Merthyr. He applied for the Swans job when Glyn Davies was appointed in succession to Trevor Morris the following year and his appointment as club coach was among the demands of the 'Ginger Group', young local businessmen including future chairman Malcolm Struel who called for a shake-up in the running of the club, in the mid 1960s. He did return, in 1967, and worked with a succession of managers before inheriting the post himself when Harry Gregg left in January 1975.

His appointment was too late to save the Swans from the shame of seeking re-election, but the week he was given the job began the revival that would culminate in topping the league less than seven years later. It also saw the club's immediate future secured by the City Council taking over the Vetch and adding a £150,000 grant to the £50,000 purchase price.

Harry had zero resources – any incomers were free transfers and he was sometimes spotted helping out in the club shop – but as Wyndham Evans recalled: "Harry told us he wanted to go out and try to play the kind of football Swansea always used to...to be creative instead of destructive".

Fun and adventure returned. In 1976–7, Harry's second full season, the Swans scored 92 league goals, a club record (although still not acknowledged in the Sky Sports Yearbook) and only missed promotion because of a 4–1 hammering by Watford in the last home match.

He did not enjoy the pressures of management and had to be dissuaded from resigning early the following season. When John Toshack was appointed, he reverted happily to the role of assistant.

In the last week of the season, the morning before the penultimate match, he collapsed and died at the Vetch Field aged 47. The players he had nurtured were devastated, but paid tribute to his memory by winning not only that night but on the following Saturday against Halifax to win promotion. As Toshack said 'if ever a man game his life for a football club, it was Harry Griffiths'.

G is also for **Giorgio Chinaglia,** who in the mid 1960s confirmed British stereotypes of continental players as gifted but lazy, temperamental and generally unreliable – earning a free transfer in 1966. He went on to play for

Lazio, Italy and the New York Cosmos. Recent attempts to take over Lazio have led to indictment for money-laundering and allegations of connection to the Mafia. If confirmed, they would appear to make him the first Swan with links to organised crime, although Frank Barson boasted in his playing days of his friendship with the Fowler brothers of Sheffield, gangsters executed for murder in 1925. The frauds committed by the unloved duo of joke former manager Kevin Cullis and highly unfunny ex-chairman Michael Lewis were anything but organised while for most fans a low point in criminality was set by former striker Dai Thomas. To be caught associating with either Cardiff or England hooligans would have been in bad taste. To do both really was a bit much.

And for **Gueret, Willy,** successor to Roger Freestone in the Swans goal from 2004 to 2007. 'Big Willy' played in the same Le Mans side as Didier Drogba and was a highly effective shot-stopper, although not always quite as assertive on crosses. He entered folklore by getting himself arrested during the celebrations that followed promotion from the Third Division at Bury in 2005 when a Greater Manchester policeman – possibly unaccustomed to the Guadeloupe accent – mistook his invitation to 'back off' for something else. Now plays for MK Dons.

Big Willy AT

H is for

Havard, William. In the 1950s the *Evening Post* reported that a new chapel in Swansea Prison had been been opened by William Havard, Bishop of St David's. It did not mention that the Bishop was back on familiar ground. Not the prison, but next door at the Vetch Field, where he had a permanent place in club history as the scorer of the Swans' first goal, for the reserves at Merthyr in September 1912. Havard never made the first team, but was more successful as a rugby forward, playing for Llanelli and Wales. Later vicar of St Mary's, Swansea, he preached a sermon denouncing 'money grubbing' in sport on the weekend when the Swans avoided relegation in 1934, and in the same year became Bishop of St Asaph's, moving to St David's in 1950. He died in 1956.

No other Swans life quite matches his, but some have excelled in other careers. Billy Beynon played both codes of rugby for Wales. Ken Jones, a member of one of Swansea's great footballing dynasties, did not make the first team at the Vetch but became a highly distinguished sportswriter equally at home in qualities or tabloids. There have also been four notable cricketers. David Foot, an RAF national service colleague, recalled that a wakeful Jim Pressdee told cheerful stories of his life at the Vetch, but in his sleep cursed Glamorgan's domineering, hard-riding captain Wilfred Wooller. Pressdee made only eight league appearances but had a fruitful cricket career, doing the double of 1000 runs and 100 wickets in 1963 and helping spin Glamorgan to victory over Australia a year later before a culminating row with Wooller precipitated emigration to South Africa in 1965. Goalkeeper Joe Hills also played eight first-team games, in the 1920s, before taking part in partnerships which still stand as Glamorgan records for the eighth and ninth wicket, while his near namesake Len Hill played for the Swans, Newport County and Glamorgan half a century later. Also more successful as a cricketer was Tony Cottey, a neat, diminutive midfielder who played three league matches before being released in 1985. A batsman close to test quality, he won

The all-rounder: Jim Pressdee

more county championships, one each with Glamorgan and Sussex, than any other Welshman.

Herbie Williams. If ever a player was born at the wrong time, it was Herbie. A few years older and he could have adorned the exciting Swans teams of the middle 1950s, and quite possibly the 1958 World Cup. Any later and he might have been part of the club's revival from the mid 1970s. Instead his career covers, with almost painful precision, the time in between.

Few Swans prospects have inspired such anticipation. Following his debut as a 17 year old inside-forward in a 5–0 win over Sunderland in 1958 *Evening Post* reporter Bill Paton, his account accompanied by the memorable headline 'Ivor and Len sparkle as Swans go gay', described him as 'a natural if ever there was one', who after a nervy start 'pinpointed passes with an uncanny accuracy'.

By the time he scored his first league goal, beating Middlesbrough keeper Peter Taylor on November 1st, Ivor had gone to Newcastle, the Vetch needed a new hero and Paton reckoned 'He could well take over the mantle of Ivor Allchurch'. Manager Trevor Morris hailed 'the greatest talent to come out of Wales since John Charles'.

A bony, angular figure he had all the ball skills and was exceptional in the air, enabling his later conversion to wing- or centre-half. He didn't, though, fulfil those early predic-

Herbie: Great talent, bad timing

tions. One explanation is poor eyesight, which made him an early footballing contact-lens wearer. More convincing, though, is that he spent his career with a club in almost endless decline. There were odd moments of hope like a superb finish to the 1961–2 season, the cup run of 1963–4 and promotion from the Fourth Division in 1969–70. Herbie contributed hugely to them all. But by the time he left in January 1975, following 515 league appearances and 102 goals, the Swans were headed for re-election. His final league match, against Scunthorpe on 18th January 1975, attracted one of the smallest ever Vetch gates, only 1,412. A more fitting finale was a hat-trick in the

5–0 midweek hammering of Kidderminster in a Welsh Cup replay, his power in the air a constant menace. So impeccable was his bad timing that he left in the very week that the council purchase of the Vetch Field and the appointment of Harry Griffiths as manager signalled the end of that long decline.

SWANSEA CITY AFC
NATIONWIDE LEAGUE DIVISION THREE

Swansea City
v
Hull City

Sat 3rd May 2003
Kick-Off 3.00pm

EAST STAND
PRICE £13
TURNSTILES 9 - 11 (GATE 4)

PLEASE SELECT UNRESERVED SEAT ON ARRIVAL

PLEASE TAKE UP YOUR POSITION 15 MINUTES BEFORE KICK-OFF
TICKET OFFICE 01792 633425 TO BE RETAINED

00055

orange

Never again....

Hull has much in common with Swansea. Both are geographically isolated, and routinely derided by people who have never visited. Rugby and football compete in both cities for support and resources, but share a modern stadium. A further link is full-back Sam Ricketts, whose sell-on fee after departing Hull City for Bolton in 2009 provided a tidy windfall. In 1999 victory over Hull at the Vetch, in a match delayed by half an hour following torrential rain, took the Swans into the Third Division playoff.

But for most fans Hull means one thing and one date – 3rd May 2003 – when the Swans came close to losing League status after a season summed up by the feat of losing at home three times to a bottom-placed team. Victory would preserve league status, any other result would have meant relegation. The Vetch was packed with a tense and terrified crowd of 9565.

Hull were safe in mid-table, but did not lie down – instead raising those levels of tension to new levels by taking a 2–1 lead midway through the first half. With the interval looming the Swans were awarded a contentious penalty. Striker James Thomas, who had put away an earlier spot-kick, kept his nerve again and it was 2–2 at the break. The first few minutes after brought relief as midfielder Lenny Johnrose forced home after a goalmouth scramble then Thomas, sent through by an astute angled pass from Jonathan Coates, completed his hat-trick with an audacious chip. The rest had an air of carnival, but the fear before the issue was settled will never be forgotten by those there, or fans forced to follow at second hand like Peter and Bethan Charles, committed to a friend's wedding and forced to rely on text messages: "By the end, half of the people at the reception was cheering the scores", they remember. The documentary produced by a Dutch television team is supposedly brilliant, but I've no desire ever to live that day again.

H is also for **Hole,** not only something the Swans have been good at getting themselves into, but also the name of yet another of the club's remarkable families. First came Billy, a lively winger in the teams of the 1920s, later owner of newsagents shops in Swansea. His elder sons Alan and Colin were on the books together in the early 1950s, but neither had a long career. Youngest son Barry emulated Billy by playing for Wales, then inheriting the newsagency chain, but his club career followed a different path via Cardiff, Blackburn and Aston Villa. He was so keen to return to Swansea that he refused to move anywhere else before signing for a club record £20,000 in 1970, but never really recaptured the creative spark that had won him 30 Wales caps.

Founding father: Billy Hole

And for **Hutchison, Tommy,** a venerable Scottish winger who did much to lighten the prevailing darkness of the mid 1980s and contributed hugely to revival later in the decade. Tommy, who once scored for both sides in an FA Cup final, attributed his ability to play well into his 40s to rarely having been injured and also the odd habit of rubbing butter into his legs. His fitness, footballing intelligence and judgment of effort were such that, while invariably the oldest man on the field, he was often at his most effective in the last 15 minutes while his close control meant that a frequent tactic under pressure was 'give it to Tommy and let him play around with it for a few minutes'. Manager for half a season following the near-bankruptcy at Christmas 1985, his 178 league matches contributed to a career total of 863, fourth on the all-time list headed by Peter Shilton (1005).

I is for

Ivor. With the greatest, most cherished Welsh sportsmen – Gareth, Lynn the Leap, Bleddyn – no surname is required. So it is with **Ivor Allchurch,** the definitive Swans hero, the right and proper choice for the statue that reminds us, amid the rather bland precincts of the Liberty Stadium, whose ground it is.

Any debate on the greatest footballer from Swansea might concede the claim of John Charles, but his legend was written with Leeds and Juventus. Ivor is without doubt the greatest Swans player.

He was the first, other than Trevor Ford, of the club's astonishing postwar efflorescence of talent, football's answer to Dublin's writers and Budapest's mathematicians. He was the last to leave, holding longest to the dream of playing in the First Division for the Swans. He went reluctantly at 29, saying 'it is now or never', and returned seven years later for three final seasons that made him a hero to the sons of his earlier fans.

'The finest inside-forward in the world'

It is a career impossible to imagine now. The differentials in reward are so great that no world-class player would stay for years with a Second Division club, however strong his attachment.

His talents, though, would have appealed in any era, a mix of the aesthetic and the visceral. He was a subtle, elegant ball-player who struck thrilling long-range goals, a creator who was a regular scorer. When he retired his 251 league goals were the most by any Welsh player. He made many more for team-mates who were often in awe of his talents.

His Swans colleague Ray Powell recalled his 'doing things with the ball that I had not seen previously and could not imagine myself ever doing. When I lobbed the ball to him, he casually took it on his chest and rolled it down on to his knee, then to his instep before returning it to me'. All this with the heavy leather boots and ball of 1950, not the user-friendly equipment of today.

Little Brother: Len in training, 1959

He was one of those players who arrives complete and mature. The London-based writer who reported his first league match at West Ham at Christmas 1949 commented on his quality, but evidently had not the slightest idea he was a 20-year old debutant. Within weeks he played brilliantly in a memorable cup-tie at Arsenal, and was hailed as potentially 'the player of the century' by Gunners boss Tom Whittaker, who had seen ample greatness in his time, unleashing the transfer speculation that would persist over the next eight years. He nearly went in 1952, when the Swans and Wolves agreed a British record fee. That move might have brought numerous medals – Wolves won three titles and the FA Cup between 1953 and 1960 – assuming his cultured style had fitted their hard-running directness. It was purely the product of financial pressures, and Ivor was evidently happy to stay once they were eased.

He was the fixed point at inside-forward around which a carousel of brilliance – Jones, Medwin, Mel Charles – rotated. From 1954 it regularly also included younger brother Len, short and stocky where Ivor was willowy, a fine winger unavoidably overshadowed who played 347 games for the Swans, and alongside Ivor in a Wales team that also included both Charles brothers.

'See you by Ivor': The Statue of Liberty   RR

Nobody has scored so consistently for so long for the Swans. Ivor's 166 league goals are a club record. In 11 full seasons he was leading scorer five times, second on a further three.

He was still a Swans player at the World Cup in Sweden in 1958. His staggering playoff volley against Hungary took Wales through to the quarter-final against Brazil. Santiago Bernabeu, president of Real Madrid, asked Wales manager Jimmy Murphy, if he could meet 'the finest inside-forward in the world'. Those active in 1958 included Didi of Brazil, Sweden's Gunnar Gren, Valentin Ivanov of the USSR, England's Johnny Haynes and Real's own Ferenc Puskas.

The move to Newcastle came soon after, and he also played for Cardiff – once scoring a hat-trick against the Swans – before returning home. He won the last of 68 Welsh caps, then a record, at 37. Closing on 40, he was leading scorer in his last two seasons, and went on playing in the Welsh League until nearly 50. Loving the game, he saw no reason to stop.

Opinion varies on the statue's quality as both art and representation. What matters most is that it is there. Younger generations in Boston, Massachusetts identify Ted Williams not as their city's greatest baseball star, but as a tunnel. Their counterparts in Swansea know Ivor as a Swans player – *the* Swans player.

I is also for **Internet,** a vital resource for fans of a club never especially skilled at communication. While the official site is considerably improved from when the welcoming headline 'Connolly's Here!' ran long after he had left the club, the main impact has been made by unofficial, fan-maintained sites. *Jackarmy. net* was essential reading during the battle to oust Tony Petty from ownership, while the real stalwart is *scfc.co.uk*, set up by Gary Martin and run in recent years by Dai Smith, its Guestbook a continuous, sometimes maddening, periodically compulsive, forum for debate on the club and its fortunes.

And for **Internazionale** of Milan, current Italian champions, twice European Cup winners and one of former clubs of Swans manager Paulo Sousa. With 51 Portuguese caps and consecutive Champions League titles with two different clubs, Juventus and Borussia Dortmund, Sousa contests with John Toshack, Jan Molby and Ron Burgess the title of Swans manager with the most impressive playing record. His management credentials are as yet less compelling, but any player saying 'show us your medals' will be doing so out of curiosity rather than as a challenge.

Earning his stripes; Paulo Sousa

J is for

James, Robbie. If Alan Curtis was the classic hero and Jeremy Charles the dynast among the holy trinity of the late 1970s and early 1980s, Robbie was easiest to identify with. He was a footballer with a visible passion for the game, easy to imagine as a North Bank regular if he had not been good enough to play.

He began incredibly young, announcing himself as a 16 year old with a thunderous 30-yard goal against Rotherham on New Year's Day 1974, and never really stopped. At 23 he could be billed as football's youngest veteran, with nearly 300 first-team appearances. He was still playing at 40, when he collapsed and died on the pitch as Llanelli's player-manager. His 782 league appearances, 484 for the Swans, were third on the all-time list – Tommy Hutchison was second – when he retired.

He played them all with vigour and purpose, epitome of the 'bustling player' who scored spectacular long-range goals, tackled with ferocity reckoned to rival team-mates Wyndham Evans and Tommy Smith and varied pinpoint distribution with the occasional miscalculation that saw team-mates chasing passes that Usain Bolt might not have caught. Barrel-chested and powerful, he could look cumbersome, but was lethally quick over five or 10 yards.

Robbie scored in bursts, a particularly cherishable patch bringing four in four matches, including two against Aston Villa to clinch league leadership, just before Christmas 1981. He was leading scorer that season with 14. While that was the only year when he led scorers outright, he was in the top three for nine seasons in a row between 1974 and

The Holy Trinity: Curt, Jeremy and Robbie celebrate at Preston

1983, consistency matched in club history only by Ivor Allchurch.

Arguably the least intrinsically gifted of the holy trinity, he made more of his gifts, playing more times in the First Division or for Wales, 47, than Curtis or Charles. His departure in 1983 was inevitable given financial problems and playing decline, but he returned in 1988 to play in Terry Yorath's promotion-winning team before departing to Bradford City in exchange with the still more ill-fated Alan Davies. He also played for Cardiff, but like Curtis was readily forgiven. There was never the slightest doubt that he was one of us.

ROBBIE JAMES
1957 ~ 1998

In Memoriam: The Liberty remembers Robbie AT

Jones, Cliff. As with the Charleses, their main rivals as the defining Swansea football dynasty, there is no doubt which was the greatest of the Joneses – winger Cliff, one of the real dazzlers in perhaps the most exciting British club team of the 20th century, the Spurs double-winners of 1961. Cliff's father Ivor was a star of the first Swans league teams in the 1920s. Uncle Bryn became the most expensive player in Britain when Arsenal paid Wolves £14,000 for him in 1938. Cliff, whose brother Bryn also played for the Swans, grew up regarding 'soccer as the only respectable way to earn a living'.

Nor was there much doubt which club he'd play for – among Swans heroes only Terry Medwin, a contemporary whose career followed similar patterns, grew up closer to the Vetch than Cliff whose childhood was spent in the Sandfields streets close to his birthplace, number 8 Beach Street.

He also followed family traditions as an inside-forward, playing part-time for the Swans while also working as an apprentice coppersmith in the dockyards. He was shocked when Joe Sykes suggested he move to the wing at Christmas 1953, but

Sandfields Flyer: Cliff Jones

it proved a characteristically shrewd ploy. Cliff was capped for Wales within a few months and his exceptional pace – Real Madrid's Paco Gento, aka 'The Flying Bicycle', was reckoned his only rival for speed – helped make him an authentically world-class winger. Also formidable in the air, Cliff – inspired both by Medwin's tales of life with Spurs and rubbing shoulders with other top players in the Army team during national service – became another player to decide that the Swans' ambitions did not match his own. He left for Spurs for £35,000, then the second-highest fee paid by a British club, in 1958. His talents were truly reflected by those medals won with Spurs, a place among the '100 League Legends' chosen in 1998 and retiring with 59 Wales caps, at the time second only to Ivor Allchurch.

J is also for **John Cornforth,** a midfielder from the north-east who led the Swans to victory in their first ever Wembley final, the 1994 Autoglass Trophy victory on penalties over Huddersfield. He received the trophy from Gorseinon-born cabinet minister Michael Howard, whose huge slice-of-melon grin suggested far greater engagement than is usual in guests of honour. Locating some Welsh ancestry also allowed him to play twice for Wales in 1995, the first Swan capped since Andy Melville five years earlier. His misfortune was that the Swans appointed Jan Molby as player-manager in 1996. There was only ever going to be room for one creative, but achingly slow, midfield playmaker, and Cornforth departed to join Barry Fry's attempt to corner the market in professional footballers at Birmingham City.

Political endorsement. Swans skipper John Cornforth clearly has the support of Cabinet minister Michael Howard (immediately above him)

K is for

Kenny Jackett. The middle man among three consecutive highly successful appointments made by the Swans board from the low-point in late 2002, a pragmatist between two apostles of stylish football, Kenny Jackett was perhaps the most imaginative choice of the trio. Brian Flynn was local by origin, Roberto Martinez by adoption. Jackett had Swans roots – his father was on the books in the 1950s – but is chiefly associated with Watford, where he won 31 Wales caps as a full-back and was briefly manager. Trained on Warwick University's football management course, he was chosen in preference to the tired carousel of supposed 'big names'. Jackett was well regarded as an assistant at Queens Park Rangers, whose fans chanted 'There's only one

Kenny Jackett (centre) with coaching staff including Colin Pascoe (second from left)   AT

Kenny Jackett', when he returned with the Swans for a League Cup tie in late 2004. The replying chorus of 'Take him back' reflected both an abysmal performance and a broader ambivalence he never fully escaped. The London accent probably did not help nor, more justifiably, did insensitive handling of the departure of several favourites.

Appointed in 2004 to counter perceived deficiencies in physicality and fitness under Flynn, Jackett adopted a more physical and direct style and had a sharp eye for good defenders – recruiting Garry Monk, Sam Ricketts and Kevin Austin. 'Physical and direct' did not, though, ever degenerate into a simple hoofball. He appreciated inherited Flynn acquisitions like Lee Trundle and Andy Robinson and critics could reasonably be told 'look at the results'. Promotion was secured on the last day of his first full season at Bury, a huge following creating a de facto home game remembered for Adrian Forbes' early goal and Willy Gueret's post-match arrest.

A second consecutive elevation was denied in 2006 only in a penalty shoot-out in the playoff final against Barnsley at the Millennium Stadium. His problems may have begun with unproductive signings that January and momentum clearly slowed in the following season, as the Swans struggled to break out of mid-table. He departed in February 2007 by mutual consent. While he did not deserve the sack, few were desperately sorry to see him go. Succeeded by Martinez, with whom he had disagreed on fundamental footballing philosophy, he recuperated as assistant at Manchester City before returning to management with Millwall, where in 2008–9 he piloted a promotion chase ending in yet another playoff final defeat.

Kiley, Tom's knee is probably the most famed and momentous body-part in the club's history. When it went in November 1955, the Swans were top of Division Two after scoring 37 goals in an 11-match unbeaten run and set for their first serious promotion challenge for 30 years at that level. *Evening Post* writer Bill Paton perhaps tempted fate by writing the day before: "Swansea Town have been more fortunate than most in the matter of injuries".

Hope evaporated rapidly from that moment. It was the point at which the limitations of club policy during the 1950s, insisting on locally-grown talent, became clear. The 'grow your own' policy had produced what many reckoned the best forward line in the Football League, but good defenders were rarer.

They were also cheaper, and a decent centre-half need not have broken the bank. The Swans signed only Tom Brown from Llanelli, a former Doncaster player who turned out to be a wing-half. Six different centre-halves were tried before Kiley returned at the end of the season. Nothing really worked. The Swans finished 10th, yet only six points out of the promotion places.

SWANSEA TOWN FOOTBALL CLUB 1953-54

LEFT TO RIGHT - BACK ROW :- THOMAS, HOLE, KILEY, EDWARDS, WILLIAMS, PRESSDEE.
FRONT ROW :- L.ALLCHURCH, B.JONES, MEDWIN, I.ALLCHURCH, C.BEECH. INSETS :- KING, CHARLES, C.JONES

Big Man at the Back: Tom Kiley towers over his team-mates

Faith was lost long before hope was extinguished. The Swans were still second when eventual champions Sheffield Wednesday visited in late January, but the crowd was only a little over 14,000. The evidence of inadequate ambition and vision was not lost on the players. Terry Medwin went to Spurs at the end of the season, beginning the inexorable break-up of the brilliant 1950s team.

Kiley, a local product who played full-back alongside Trevor Ford for Swansea Schools before the war, had been a key figure. While he lacked the brilliance of some team-mates, at 31 he was a vital, mature influence, a centre-half like predecessor Reg Weston who exuded stability not just as a defender, but in personality. He retired after the following season. He maintained interest in the club and supported the Ginger Group of would-be reformers in the 1960s, but spent more of his later life – he died in 2000 – at St Helens than the Vetch.

K is also for **King, Johnny.** A Rhondda product who kept goal from 1950 to 1964, making 368 first-team appearances – one as an emergency centre-forward – and was good enough to explain why the Swans left it to Arsenal to persuade Jack Kelsey he had a future beyond Winch Wen. Though the goals

In Safe Hands: Johnny King

Last Ditch: Rory Keane's spectacular, penalty-conceding save at Highbury, 1950

against column does him few favours, he is generally the older fan's answer when asked if the Swans ever had a keeper as good as Roger Freestone. Like Freestone, King won a single Welsh cap, against England in 1955. Emigrating to Australia, he died there are the age of 48. For all his qualities, he never quite managed a save as memorably photogenic as full-back **Keane, Rory,** one of the Swans' postwar crop of Irish internationals, in the FA Cup tie at Arsenal in 1950, who was pictured in most national newspapers punching the ball from under the crossbar at Highbury.

L is for

Latchford, Bob. While the mental highlights reel from the Swans' First Division years is full of brilliant and spectacular goals like Gary Stanley's screamer against Man City and Alan Curtis's solo from halfway against Southampton, no team can live on such strikes alone. They also need the simple and less memorable – but still precisely as valuable – scores supplied by being in the right place and finishing calmly. In those two years the designated supplier was Bob Latchford. His signing from Everton in the 1981 close season indicated ambition beyond mere First Division survival. He was an

Bob Latchford

established star, a recent England player who three years earlier had scored 30 First Division goals. His debut hat-trick against Leeds, three goals in the first 11 minutes after half-time, each a model of calmly composed finishing, made him an instant hero. He went on to score 12 goals, combine to often lethal effect with Alan Curtis and play one of the essential roles in John Toshack's innovative tactical scheme, the single striker playing a little forward of other attackers. He was well equipped for this by ability to hold and shield possession in crowded penalty areas and in particular his brilliance with the ball above waist height, using chest and upper body to control. His second season was, in personal terms, even more impressive. The Swans fell apart, not least through injuries – midfield organiser John Mahoney broke an ankle, Curtis missed 29 games and skipper Colin Irwin hardly played again – and were relegated. This was no fault of Latchford who scored 20 goals in 28 games. He departed before Christmas the following season, but left only good memories.

Lee Trundle. *Lee, Lee, Lee Trundle* in North Bank and East Stand choruses, and LT10 to internet polemicists, the defining, dominating on-field personality of the time that saw recovery from the low point of 2002–3 and the transition from Vetch to Liberty.

Lee, Lee, Lee Trundle, complete with trophy   RR

Brought from Wrexham by Brian Flynn, Trundle was an original, eccentric talent whose exuberant delight in his own skills reflected a late conversion to the duller disciplines of the professional game. A poser, a wind-up merchant and a diver – eventually referees became so wary that legitimate claims were rejected along with the Greg Louganis impersonations – he was, unlike most such players, a hard worker as aware of better-placed team-mates as of his own opportunities. Musings as to what he might accomplish if he were quicker – the name was highly appropriate – or had a decent right foot were rapidly succeeded by recognition that under either circumstance he would hardly have joined a team that had just finished 90th in the league. His peculiar talents also made it difficult to find an effective partner – ideally they needed to be big and quick, a combination rarely found, at least for long, among lower-league strikers. The best was the similarly unorthodox Bayo Akinfenwa.

Trundle announced his arrival with consummate swagger and a well-taken goal in the opening day victory over Bury at the Vetch in August 2003, then attained instant North Bank Idol status with a second-half comeback that brought the Swans back from 3–1 down to win 4–3 at Cheltenham – not previously a fruitful hunting ground – in the match that also saw the first appearance of his fellow-Scouser and late developer Andy Robinson. Acutely one-footed he may have been, but he could use it to feint, shuffle and shape a shot so distinctively that before long most fans could recognise a Trundle strike, like the extraordinary chip from halfway that struck the crossbar at the end of a epic 4–2 loss at Southend, by trajectory alone. He scored remarkable goals like the instinctive 40 yard lobbed return of a poor clearance by Yeovil in front of the Liberty's record football crowd, or the opener in the League Trophy final victory over Carlisle. The goals came with quantity as well as quality, 77 in 143 league matches, topping 20 in consecutive years and never dropping below 16.

Liverpool origins were evident both in distaste for Yorkshire – he was sent off at York and Huddersfield – and squeaky tones that became nationally known through his appearances on Sky's *Soccer A.M.* Those TV appearances underpinned fame that earned him a celebrity partner – Atomic Kitten's Liz MacLarnon – and an intellectual property deal, unique for a lower division player, on his huge proportion of club shop sales. Awareness of advancing age and a desire to play for the Republic of Ireland eventually persuaded him to seek a move to Bristol City in August 2007. Persistent rumours of his return came to fruition in a loan deal, and reincarnation as LT19, two years later.

Liverpool. If Everton have rarely been good news, associations with the red half of Liverpool are – matching Swansea's political traditions – much happier. The FA Cup quarter-final victory of 1964, when bottom-of-the-Second-Division Swans upset league leaders Liverpool 2–1 at Anfield thanks to goals by Jimmy McLaughlin and Eddie Thomas, and goalkeeper Noel Dwyer playing the match of his life, is probably the best moment in a chequered association with the tournament.

Later came the Toshack era when the footballing principles he imbibed at Anfield and imports either directly from Liverpool – Ian Callaghan, Tommy Smith, Colin Irwin – or with previous like Phil Boersma and Alan Waddle – contributed much to the club's spectacular rise. The sole drawback was a media tendency to attribute it solely to the Liverpool connection, ignoring both Harry Griffiths and Toshack's inheritance of local talent. The league trip to Liverpool in 1981 saw the first serious misstep of Toshack's career. It was perhaps understandable, returning to Anfield only a few days after Bill Shankly's death, that Toshack wore a Liverpool top during the minute's

SWANSEA CITY 1980-81

Back row: Wyndham Evans, David Giles, Glan Letheren, David Stewart, Brian Attley.
Middle row: Terry Medwin (Assistant Manager), Leighton James, John Mahoney, Chris Marustik, Alan Waddle, Nigel Stevenson, Neil Robinson, Phil Boersma (Trainer-Coach)
Seated: Ian Callaghan, Tommy Craig, Leighton Phillips, John Toshack (Manager), Jeremy Charles, Robbie James, Dave Rushbury.

Ex-Anfield men in the 1981 promotion squad included Alan Waddle (tallest in middle row), Ian Callaghan (front, far left), John Toshack (front centre) and trainer Phil Boersma (middle, far right)

silence and saluted the Kop post-match. If only he had similarly greeted his own fans, packed none too comfortably into the away section, after the 2–2 draw. He was after all our manager, not theirs, and the Swans were several places higher up the league.

Since then, though, Liverpool have proved understanding creditors when Colin Irwin's transfer fee was one of the debts threatening the club's existence in 1985, and – before inflicting a club record 8–0 defeat in the FA Cup in 1990 – allowed the 0–0 draw at the Vetch that gave the Swans a much-needed replay payday and keeper Lee Bracey his 15 minutes of fame. Jan Molby's managership – and accent – renewed the acquaintance in the later 1990s, and in 2008 the Swans did themselves a lot of good by not playing Liverpool. Any envy watching cup conquerors Havant and Waterlooville taking the lead at Anfield was leavened by the comforting reflection that getting knocked out allowed the Swans to play their scheduled league fixture and produce the key performance of a triumphant year, a 4–0 win at Doncaster, the second best team in League One.

Leighton James' spectacular opener at Preston in 1981

L is also for **Leighton,** a forename that has fallen largely into disuse, but is forever associated with two important figures of the Toshack era. First to arrive, in 1978 was **Leighton Phillips**, an elegant, ball-playing Welsh international centre-back from Aston Villa who lost form – and with it Toshack's confidence – in the 1981 promotion run, but not before supplying class and composure in 97 appearance across three seasons. He coincided for a year with **Leighton James,** one of the best of the local boys who got away – like Brian Flynn, to Burnley – a brilliantly mercurial winger famously told by Tommy Docherty that he was deceptive because he was 'slower than he looked'. Two goals stand out from the 27 he scored in a productive time with the Swans – the wide-angled curler that opened the scoring in the promotion-clincher at Preston and a rocketing free-kick from a fast bowler's run up in the 2–0 Vetch victory over Liverpool the following season. Not to be confused with **Leyton Orient.**

M is for

Manager and in particular three who, in widely differing styles, brought some success to the Vetch – **Bill McCandless, Trevor Morris** and **Jan Molby.** McCandless, remembered by Cliff Jones as 'short but immensely broad...a good practical manager', in 1949 completed an astonishing hat-trick, taking the three southern Welsh clubs to the Third Division South championship inside four seasons, and managed until he died in 1955. Morris, who came from Cardiff in 1958, was a transfer wheeler-dealer and astute tactician who took the Swans to the FA Cup semi-final in 1964, but was fired following relegation to the Third Division a year later. Each lasted seven years. Molby's 20 months was more typical of recent times. The Dane jokingly known as 'the only Scouser in the team' at Liverpool encouraged good football and remained an on-field force himself, but had uncertain judgment over trans-fers, lost the 1997 playoff final and was fired when Doug Sharpe tired of

his propensity for heckling his chairman much as he did referees. His was a renewal of the player-manager tradition represented by John Toshack, Ron Burgess (1955–8) – a better player than coach – and, as emer-gency stand-ins, Tommy Hutchison and Nick Cusack.

The Swans also won promotion under their first league manager Joe Bradshaw and two ex-Chelsea notables, Roy Bentley and John Hollins. The last divided opinion more than most. He was averse to the transfer market and defensively-minded. One inter-net poster thought he 'put the club back 10 years'. In fact he put it back 20, to a time when it won things, taking the Third Division title in 2000 with an extremely limited team that was rapidly exposed a league higher.

At the other end of the scale are the incredibly brief terms of office of Kevin Cullis, exposed in league managerial terms as a fraud

Three times a winner: Bill McCandless

Future Swans manager Roy Bentley (right) tussles for possession with Mel Charles

roughly a decade before he was convicted of the financial version, and Micky Adams, a proven boss who fell out with club owners Silver Shield within days – and three over-promoted deputies in Ian Evans, Bobby Smith and Alan Cork. That four of these five managed the Swans in a three-year period also covering Molby's tenure illustrates the chaos between 1995 and 1998. More durable but no more successful were Glyn Davies, whose overtrained squad were already well on the way to relegation when he was sacked 13 games into the 1966–7 season and Harry Gregg, responsible for new lows in performance and discipline. Unluckiest manager was probably Colin Addison who, along with Odd Couple assistant Peter Nicholas – 20 years younger but looking 20 older – cleared the chaos left by detested owner Tony Petty in 2002 but walked out when told that the club could not afford to renew his contract.

Martinez, Roberto. He was supposed to be our Arsene Wenger or Dario Gradi, the manager who encourages great football and raises the standing of a club by his long-term influence. The shock of his departure for Wigan in the summer of 2009 was immense, and is likely to ripple for some time.

No Swans manager has inspired quite such faith and affection. John Toshack was revered, but never exactly lovable. Martinez was not only universally liked, but started with the advantages of the popular recent player.

As a player he was perhaps the most important of the relief convoy of loanees summoned by Brian Flynn to fight against relegation to the Conference in 2002–3. A neat, thoughtful midfield playmaker, he acted as a brain transfusion for a previously bemused team. Room-mate Leon Britton was impressed by his authority,

Wigan's gain: Roberto in tactical debate with Ferrie Bodde

experience and habit of reading books, behaviour he had evidently not encountered at West Ham.

The natural captain under Flynn, he fared less well under Jackett, his marginalisation most obvious when not used even as a substitute – when his control and composure might have made all the difference – in the playoff final against Barnsley.

It says much for both him and Jackett that their philosophical differences were not aired publicly. He was released in 2006, but returned from Chester a few months later as Jackett's successor. It was an imaginative appointment – betting what the board knew of his character and intelligence against his lack of managerial experience.

It could hardly have worked better. He proved an astute transfer-market operator in partnership with chief scout Kevin Reeves. Martinez was also a sharp tactician whose best single decision was probably the conversion of Britton into a holding midfielder and a passionate advocate of football based on possession, passing and movement.

In a period when Spanish football was both fashionable and successful, the Swans became offshore exemplars of the same style and values. The League One title in 2008 was followed by establishing themselves in the top half of the Championship, rivalled for style only by Burnley and Doncaster, equalling their best League Cup run and going further in the FA Cup than since 1965. The 2009 team could claim to be the third best in club history, behind only the 1926 Cup semi-finalists and the 1980–2 Toshack teams, eighth place a genuine over-achievement in relation to resources.

Martinez made much of a genuine affinity with club and city, once saying 'I'll have to be forced out of here, like I was as a player'. There were, though, always two threats to a lasting relationship. One was the Really Big Job, the other an approach from Wigan, which had a rival call on his emotions as the first club he'd played for in England. The anger that followed his departure, along with most of his backroom including Reeves, had a strong echo of the rejected lover: 'I thought you were different, but you're just like all the rest'. He left a job unfinished and a fear that the budget version of Barcelona might easily become just another middle-division struggler.

Medwin, Terry. Among Swansea's sporting heroes only the rugby-playing Bancroft brothers, born in their grandfather's groundsman's house at St Helens's, outpoint Terry Medwin in proximity of birthplace to the ground where they became famous. Terry was born in Swansea Prison, across the road from the Vetch, giving the Swans good reason to thank the prison service for posting Terry's father, previously a professional with Southampton, to Swansea as a warder. While older by a couple of years his career ran in close

TERRY MEDWIN
SWANSEA TOWN F.C.
1954

Local boy made good: Terry Medwin

parallel with another very local hero, Cliff Jones, both working as dockyard apprentices, making their league debuts in 1952 and rapidly progressing to play for Wales. Each, in the style of the brilliant young Swans forwards of the time, could play more than one position. Terry's 147 appearances for the Swans included time at wing, inside-forward and centre-forward and produced 57 goals. He filled the number nine shirt during the spectacular start to the 1955–6 season, finishing as leading scorer with 18 goals. His range of skills made him a centre-forward in a more modern idiom, holding and distributing well and creating chances for others, rather than the head-down charger on goal typical of the age. His departure for Spurs at the end of the season, the first major sale since Roy Paul six years earlier, represented in retrospect the beginning of the end of the dream of taking the Swans into the First Division with homegrown talent. His gifts were to prove particularly well suited to the brilliant team constructed by Bill Nicholson at Spurs in the late fifties and early sixties, winning a Championship medal in 1961 and playing in the Cup final victory over Burnley a year later.

He returned in 1978, becoming John Toshack's assistant in succession to Harry Griffiths and a significant figure as the club finally achieved the dream that had proved beyond it in his days as a player. He summed up the sense of wonder felt by long-term fans and old players after the victory at Preston that clinched promotion in 1981, when he said: "I left Swansea 25 years ago to play in the First Division….Players won't have to leave Swansea to play in the First Division now."

M is also for **Melville, Andy** and **Monk, Garry,** two centre-backs who might have made fine, complementary pairing had they been the same age. It was more than just the moustache that reminded Liverpool fans who saw the young Melville of Mark Lawrenson – there were also comfort on the ball, positional sense and time to spare. Those qualities earned him 61 Wales caps, the first with the Swans before he left in 1990, and sustained him as a Premier League defender into his late 30s. Monk, a decade younger, came from

Are you sure this new set-piece routine will work? Garry Monk (top) reaches for the sky AT

Southampton in 2004 as one of Kenny Jackett's most important signings and remains a key figure two managers on. A powerful stopper-type centre-back, he is prone to mishap in the form of own goals and red cards, but is also a leader and organiser never more appreciated than when absent.

And for **Myra Powles,** presiding deity of the club shop when it was the converted front room of a small terraced house in William Street, purveyor of programmes, match tickets, scarves and other souvenirs. As with other facilities, space and comfort have been gained at the expense of character and distinctiveness in the move to the Liberty.

N is for

North Bank, whose place in collective memory is demonstrated every time 'I'll stand here on the North Bank until the day I die', is sung at the Liberty Stadium four years – and counting – after that promise was irrevocably broken. It will probably be sung long after anybody remembers standing at football matches. The North Bank was to the Vetch what the Kop was to Anfield or the Holte End to Villa Park – the ground's heartbeat, its voicebox, principal source of its atmosphere and of noise levels to rival anything in British football. Unlike them, it was along the side rather than the end of the ground, a function of the peculiarly cramped geography of the Vetch – too hemmed in by the houses of William and Richardson Streets on two sides, and the prison and drill hall on the third, to allow substantial development anywhere

Heartbeat of the Vetch: The North Bank seen from the East Stand   RR

As We Remember It: Standing Room Only AT

else. Only the North side, particularly once the Vetch Field school was closed and demolished in 1925, permitted depth as well as height. Initially it was primitive – some might say it never ceased to be – an accumulation of ash and other waste partially tamed by railway sleepers.

Until 1951, when it was still as likely to be referred to as the Main or Popular Bank, it was entered by the simple expedient of walking around the side – creating what surveyors called a 'dangerous corner' – or scrambling over the top. Only then was the back walled off and an entry tunnel created, followed in 1959 by a roof funded through a £16,000 Supporters Club dona-tion. While the crowds sheltered thereafter were smaller in number, they were more comfortable – rain is not unknown between August and May in South Wales – and at half-time could move along the bank towards the end the Swans were attacking in the second half.

Successive ground safety acts cut its capacity, with a barrier eventually sealing off sections at the back. Nothing, though, diminished its ambience – while fans at the back found that beating on the barrier added percus-sion accompaniment to terrace anthems. Rather less missed is the redbrick *tŷ bach* that served the Bank, a fearsomely noxious Black Hole in which handwashing was considered an unnecessary luxury, rated the worst toilet in British football – no mean claim – two years running by a BBC sports programme.

Mel: the early years

Nurse, Mel. To help save a club once makes you a hero. To do it twice, particularly if you are already a popular ex-player, takes you into the stratosphere. Mel Nurse – centre-half, businessman and hotelier – can claim all of this following his role first among supporters of Doug Sharpe's campaign to rescue the club 1985–6, then as the public face of the struggle to eject Tony Petty in 2001–2. Yet without any of this, he would still be a popular figure. His emergence as a solid young centre-half who idolised team-mate Ivor Allchurch came just too late for the mid-1950s teams who needed only a little more defensive stability to be serious promotion contenders. He had physical presence, football skills and a combative streak that led a reminiscing Brian Clough to describe him, not without affection, as a 'dirty bugger'.

Sharing Bobby Charlton's birthdate of October 11th 1937, he might have become his team-mate when Manchester United offered £30,000 in 1960, but remained at the Vetch, the subject of consistent transfer rumours, until his departure to Middlesbrough in September 1962. His return in 1968 saw a sharp, and hardly coincidental, decline in the goals-against tally and together with another prodigal, Len Allchurch, he contributed hugely to winning promotion to the Third in 1970. He also came close to a great cup exploit, dominating Leeds United's strike force in an FA Cup tie at Elland Road only, like many players who faced Leeds in that period, to retaliate against calculated provocation. Without their leader, the Swans lost 2–1 to a late goal. He retired from league football in 1971, manager Roy Bentley reckoning that losing him and Len, who went at the same time, began the decline towards relegation two years later. His final total was 256 league appearances and 11 goals, his most important contribution still to come.

N is also for **Nuneaton, Northampton and Nemesis** – all much the same thing. Nuneaton Borough inflicted the Swans' first FA Cup defeat by a non-league club in 1966, then repeated the trick in 1993. They have though, been replaced in nightmares since the 1997 Wembley playoff final by Northampton and the image of John Frain's retaken free-kick – with the ball moved by a referee who refused to allow the wall to adjust – screaming past Roger Freestone with so little time left that the Swans hardly got to kick off. Subsequent trips to their Sixfields stadium saw two goals conceded in injury time in 2001 and the worst display of the triumphant 2007–8 season. Two divisions separate the clubs in 2009–10, not remotely enough for peace of mind.

O is for

Official Receiver. Football clubs are astonishingly resilient organisms, the wonder being that more do not go under. Even so the Receiver has frequently loomed large. One crisis was averted in 1975 by Swansea City Council purchasing the Vetch for £50,000 and adding a grant of £150,000.

Undoubtedly the closest brush was on Friday 20th December 1985, when the High Court granted an Inland Revenue winding-up order. The Third Division match against Walsall scheduled the day after at the Vetch, was postponed and manager John Bond sacked. Campaigns to save the club began immediately and a three-week stay of execution was granted on appeal. On Boxing Day a team picked by Tommy Hutchison and Jimmy Rimmer fulfilled the fixture with Cardiff at Ninian Park. Collecting boxes were out – with many Cardiff fans contributing – with the sense of 'where there's life there's hope' only slightly dampened by Nigel Vaughan's late winner for Cardiff.

Doug Sharpe's (behind banner, dark suit) finest hour. The High Court, 1986

Fundraising and court battles lasting several months concluded success-fully on 20th July 1986, Doug Sharpe's finest hour, as Mr Justice Hoffman congratulated him on his persistence and energy in the club's cause. Relegation scarcely mattered – at least there was still a club to be relegated.

Both Hoffman and Mr Justice Scott, who granted the stay of execution, later became law lords. Mr Justice Harman, who agreed the winding-up order and accused the club of stealing from the Inland Revenue, further displayed his affinity for football in 1990 by asking 'who is Gazza?' and resigned in 2004 after an inquiry found him guilty of 'weakening public confidence in the whole judicial process'. He was voted worst judge in the country, judicial equivalent of the North Bank toilets, three years running by *Legal Business* magazine.

His removal came as the Swans were emerging from a second brush with the receiver, with the conclusion of the Company Voluntary Agreement under which they had operated since 2002. Granted following the departure of previous owners Ninth Floor Ltd and the fan campaign to oust carpetbagger Tony Petty, the device – which seeks creditor agreement to accept a proportion of what they are owed – has been widely used by football clubs. The Swans' good fortune was that theirs came before the league began to impose the points penalties that devastated, among others, Wrexham.

Orange. Colour of a 1990s away shirt of such hideousness that Swans fans for years after were asked 'what was it with those orange shirts?'. While it is possible to ruin even a white shirt – the 2009–10 edition is chief exhibit for the prosecution – more creativity has generally gone into the variegated colour schemes displayed on away grounds. Some have not been that bad – you did not have to be from Neath or New Zealand to appreciate the all black change strip worn for some seasons.

What were they thinking? Pic: David Szabo

Orange is also the colour worn by the Swans' current Dutch imports on international age-group appearances. Goalkeeper Dorus de Vries and midfielder Ferrie Bodde, previously team-mates at Den Haag, both arrived at the Liberty in the summer of 2007, De Vries via a two-year diversion to Dunfermline. De Vries has been consistent, a fine-shot stopper and brave, returning after a ghastly facial injury late in 2008 to play some matches with a face mask. That this was his only significance absence is just as well – for most

of the time he has been the only senior goalkeeper. A little prone to moments of 'after you, Ashley, no after…oh ****' at set-pieces, he was also famed for not saving penalties until the opening day of 2009–10 at Leicester.

The crewcut Bodde arrived billed as 'Holland's Roy Keane', a reputation he has upheld as a midfield driving force who hits magnificent 40-metre passes, scores spectacular long-range goals – his effort against Preston in late 2008 would make an all-time Swans highlight reel – and is periodically sent off, notably for a fearsome tackle on a Leeds player at

Agent Orange: Dorus considers his options AT

Rocket strike: Ferrie Bodde prepares to fire on goal AT

Christmas 2007. A cruciate injury late in 2008 ended his involvement early last season, but did little to halt continuous transfer speculation. Any attraction to the vast sums mentioned is considerably lessened by the requirement to pass on half to Den Haag as a sell-on fee. The cruciate injury recurred in September 2009, ruling him out for another season.

Orange is also the colour, whatever their fans tell you, worn by Blackpool, who produced perhaps the best performance yet seen at the Liberty, winning 6–3 on the final day of the 2006–7 season.

O is also for **O'Leary, Kristian.** Epitome of the limited trier, a local lad who has played 284 matches over 14 seasons and sealed himself in collective affection in 2007 when he turned down a three-year deal with Cheltenham to sign for a shorter period at the Liberty. A 'not quite' player just short of the passing ability needed in midfield or the height for a central defender, but

Onward Kristian Soldier: O'Leary, battling as always   AT

never found wanting for effort and a fiercely effective tackler. Cherished for these qualities by Kenny Jackett, his departure has often been forecast, but is yet to happen, under his successors.

And for **Orient,** an East London club prone to frequent changes of name – becoming Leyton rather than Clapton Orient in 1946, dropping Leyton in 1966 and reapplying it in 1987 – who have recently disguised their Brisbane Road ground as a housing development. They also have the inherent like-ability of smaller London clubs. As with Brentford, nearby options offer much more scope for the antisocial jerk. One question constantly asked by football fans is 'how big is my club?'. One measure is to find who most resembles you. For Swans, in historic terms at least, it is Orient. Our highs have been slightly higher – two top-flight seasons and two FA Cup semi-finals to their one of each – but our lows are also a little lower. Eighteen level four seasons with two bottom four finishes, compares to their 15 and one – although they also had some unhappy years in the old Third South. Orient have had more second-level seasons, 41 to 36, but the first 11 were before the Swans joined the league in 1920 while their 36 third-level seasons compare to the Swans' 27. There is much in common with clubs like Bradford City, Plymouth, Bury and Millwall – Bury's history since 1920 is particularly like ours, but the overall balance is seriously tipped by their two earlier FA Cup victories – but nobody as much as the three incarnations of the Orient. That conclusion is under-lined by head to head results over 36 seasons – making them the second most frequent league opponent, tied with Bristol Rovers and Brentford and one season ahead of Bury – which shows Orient leading by 28 wins to 27, with 17 draws. None of those meetings is more fondly recalled than the last visit to Brisbane Road in late 2007, the first serious hint of the League One title charge that followed as Orient, then top of the table, were hammered 5–0.

And also **Ospreys,** rugby-playing groundsharers at the Liberty Stadium. An occasionally uneasy joining of the forces of Neath and Swansea – both Blackjacks and All Greys were jokingly suggested as alternative names – the Ospreys sell thousands of replica shirts and have a hugely talented squad full of Welsh Grand Slam winners and British Lions including Shane Williams, Ryan Jones and Gavin Henson, but attract smaller average crowds than the Swans and have so far failed the defining test of the Heineken Cup.

P is for

Paul, Roy. That good players leave is a part of being a lower division club with a record of generating prime talent. Nobody, though, left Swansea quite like club captain Roy Paul in 1950. That summer he joined players attracted to Colombia by high wages offered by rebel clubs outside FIFA jurisdiction. Nobody was more surprised than Mrs Paul, who thought her husband was in Blackpool. Paul was rapidly disillusioned, a state of mind mirrored by the club on his return. He never played for the Swans again, but was sold to Manchester City for £18,000, then a sizeable fee. His finest moment there was lifting the FA Cup after the 1956 final, best remembered for City goalkeeper Bert Trautmann playing on with a broken neck.

Paul, a Rhondda native born in 1920, was rescued from the pit by signing for the Swans in 1938. He waited eight years, including war service as a PT instructor in the marines and threats by manager Bill McCandless to send him back to the mines unless he speeded up, for his league debut in

Big in Bogota: The classic wing-half

the first postwar match against West Bromwich Albion. Both as an individual and alongside Reg Weston and Frank Burns in an outstanding half-back line, he was the defining presence at the Vetch between the departure of Trevor Ford in 1946 and the rise of Ivor Allchurch in 1950. Paul was a classical wing-half, a skilled ball-player and immaculate distributor, reckoned by the astute and knowledgeable Cliff Jones to be one of the best Welsh players of his time. He was also tough and aggressive, wont to lead with a brandished fist. His book *A Red Dragon of Wales* preaches traditional masculinity, complaining of 'namby-pamby tendencies' creeping into the game and vehemently criticising continental playing styles and standards of sportsmanship. In later life he drove a lorry, but the Vetch was reminded of his talents via the comparable skills, and more genial personality, of his nephew Alan Curtis.

Petty, Tony. Clowns, jokers, misers, incompetents – the Swans board-room has seen them all, but precious few pantomine villains. Tony Petty, an Australian-based Londoner who controlled the club for a few months after buying it from chairman Michael Lewis for £1 in late 2001, heads the list. His precise purpose never became clear. He certainly showed a staggering ignorance of labour law – not even in post-Thatcherite Britain can you sack seven contracted employees without notice or compensation – and a genius for public relations that rapidly united an entire community against him. He was little seen at the club, running it through a placeman with a past in the porn industry. When he did visit, those who met him reported him not as nice as his image, and bemused opponents Rushden and Diamonds found themselves almost an irrelevance as the entire Vetch crowd barracked him for 90 minutes. Manager Colin Addison remembered him as 'an idiot'. Player representative Nick Cusack and Mel Nurse, symbolic leader of the local con-sortium aiming to reclaim the Swans, became local heroes in a struggle that included a rare fixture fans wanted the club to lose – when Petty, Swansea City FC in legal terms at this point, was challenged in the High Court. He could claim that he benefited the club by uniting all factions in the quest against a common enemy and stimulating the growth of the Swansea City Supporters Trust, but would still be ill-advised to advance this argument any-where in West Wales.

Playoffs. Given the propensity during the Toshack years for obtaining promotion via the scenic route – going into the last 15 minutes of each of the three triumph-ant seasons with the final issue still in doubt – the Swans were always going to seize the opportunity for further prolonging the agony invented in 1987.

The first experience, within 12 months, was misleadingly happy. The Swans squeezed into the final Fourth Division playoff place, winning the last two matches as four rivals fell over themselves, went to Torquay United for the second leg of the final, led 5–2 on aggregate and then had to hang on desperately for victory by the odd goal. With only 350 Swans fans allowed into Torquay's tiny ground this remains one of the true rarities in 'I was there' bragging contests. The result transformed an essentially mediocre season – the Swans won only three more league matches than they lost – into a good one.

Four subsequent excursions have shown the truer face of the playoffs, a means by which good seasons end feeling as if you have been relegated. In 43 distinctly chequered years as a fan, nothing matches the Third Division playoff final against Northampton at Wembley in 1997 for unmitigated ghastliness. The match was abysmal, their winning goal both contentious and agonisingly late. Northampton, thanks largely to manager Ian Atkins, were graceless, gloating winners. The loss to Barnsley in the League One

Latest in a long line of disappointments

final in 2006, even with the added tantalisation of extra-time and penalties, did not seem nearly as bad.

One reason for the Swans' insipidity against Northampton was that a horrible semi-final injury to full-back Steve Jones forced David Penney, the driver of the midfield, back into defence. Ill-timed injury, ruling out the speedily incisive Jason Bowen, also blighted hopes in the 1993 playoff semi-final against West Brom better remembered for Andy McFarlane's own goal – with the Swans 2–0 up and Albion rocking – at the Vetch and Colin West's sending-off just as fortunes appeared to be changing at the Hawthorns. An ill-timed work commitment made me the first visitor to Prague who really wanted to be in West Bromwich. Memorable action in the 1999 semi-final against Scunthorpe was crammed into extra-time at Glanford Park, with the Swans first behind, then ahead on away goals, then finally, definitively, behind. The pleasure of three subsequent promotions by the direct route has been accentuated by the reflection 'thank God, no playoffs'.

Preston North End share much more than white shirts with the Swans. Two meetings, separated by 17 years, make each the other's version of Kipling's twin impostors. For older fans the 1964 FA Cup semi-final remains the supreme disappointment. For the middle-aged, the league match at Deepdale in 1981 is an unmatched triumph.

The first was the zenith of the club's FA Cup achievement. The 1926 semi-final was rapidly ended as a contest by three early Bolton goals. Hope lasted much longer in the all-Second Division semi 38 years later, making despair much more acute. In torrential rain at Villa Park, the Swans adjusted more rapidly, taking the lead through Northern Irish international Jimmy McLaughlin.

At half-time most Swans fans believed they were 45 minutes from Wembley. Instead Preston equalised from a penalty Swans manager Trevor Morris described as 'diabolical', then won with a thump forward from the centre-circle by centre-half Tony Singleton. Coming out of what one Preston fan remembers as 'the lowest cloud ever seen in Aston', it caught keeper Noel Dwyer – hero of the quarter-final victory over Liverpool – out of position. Singleton failed to score in 286 league appearances and said at the time: "I did not mean to score. I just tried to get the ball back into the Swansea goalmouth as quickly as possible".

The Swans have not progressed beyond the fifth round since, and were relegated in 1965, ending a 40-year spell in which only two seasons were spent outside Division Two. Preston's 3–2 loss to West Ham is remembered as one of the better finals, but nor have they been back.

For veterans of Villa Park, there was more than just a first ever promotion to Division One at stake at Deepdale on 3rd May 1981. The wooden floor of the Town End shook for the entire 90 minutes under the feet of a huge, noisy Swans contingent. Nerves were settled by a fine start

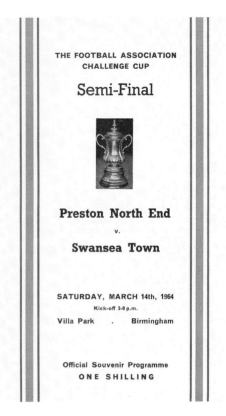

THE FOOTBALL ASSOCIATION
CHALLENGE CUP

Semi-Final

Preston North End

v.

Swansea Town

SATURDAY, MARCH 14th, 1964
Kick-off 3-0 p.m.

Villa Park . Birmingham

Official Souvenir Programme
ONE SHILLING

The day before the Ides of March, and just as dangerous

as Leighton James curled an exquisite shot round the Preston keeper, then Tommy Craig added a second. For once it seemed a final day might be routine then, with 10 minutes to go, Alex Bruce pulled one back. Preston pressed forward with the desperation of a team playing for survival, prompting several minutes of panic. Then with three minutes to go three men who had been with the Swans from the start of their rise combined. Alan Curtis broke on the right and crossed to Robbie James who drew the final defender and sent Jeremy Charles in at an angle on goal. Charles finished and promotion was secured. It was momentous for Preston too. They fell out of the top two divisions and took the best part of 20 years to get back.

If not quite as historic, recent meetings with Preston mean younger fans also have happy memories. The double attained by two of the best performances of the 2008–9 season followed an FA Cup victory in 2004, secured by a typical Lee Trundle goal, controlling with his chest before shimmying and firing home.

Toshack strikes a vital equaliser 1979

And for **Plymouth Argyle,** the Swans' most frequent league opponents. The 2009–10 season will be the 40th in which they have met. Plymouth lead 31–30 with 17 matches drawn. Late season draws at Home Park in 1925 and 1979, the latter the Swans first appearance on *Match of the Day*, were essential to winning promotion to Division Two. Wins at the Vetch in 1934 and 1962 helped avert relegation from it. Destination for popular goalkeepers, Noel Dwyer and Geoff Crudgington, and for winger Barrie Jones, the best local product of the 1960s, Plymouth in return provided the Swans with 1920s goalscoring hero Jack Fowler. In 1936 the Swans played Plymouth away on Good Friday and at home on Easter Monday. In between, on the Saturday, they visited Newcastle United, the League compensating for a monster fixture foul-up by paying for a sleeper car on the train.

And **Pratley, Darren,** a tough, athletic midfielder pursued by Kenny Jackett over a couple of seasons, in one of them playing against the Swans for Brentford in a playoff semi-final. The tenacious midfield presence lacking since the departure of Lenny Johnrose, he also developed as an attacker under Roberto Martinez, with his ability to get ahead of Jason Scotland and offer a further attacking option one of the key determinants of Swans performance. Injury cost him a first cap for Jamaica in early 2009, then ruled him out of the start of the 2009–10 season.

Q is for

Queen of the South, from whom the Swans bought striker Steve Dobbie, latest in a long line of Scots and Irishmen to play for the club, in the summer of 2009. The Scots number around 40 compared to 30 or so Irishmen, evenly divided between North and Republic. Scots proliferated before the Second World War, with Jock Denoon and Alex Ferguson (no, not that one) between them making 453 appearances in goal between 1920 and 1936. The spectacular success of the 1924–6 period coincided with the arrival from Notts County of Lachlan McPherson, who played 199 games before earning a club record £6,000 from Everton.

The great Irish influx came immediately after the war with manager Haydn Green astutely exploiting a source of players akin to modern Scandinavians – English-speaking and less expensive than home-based talent. There were five – Jim Feeney, Rory Keane, Norman Lockhart, Sam McCrory and Jack O'Driscoll – at the club at the beginning of 1947–8 and all but Lockhart were regulars in the Third Division South winning team the following season. Feeney, Keane and O'Driscoll were capped while with the Swans but McCrory had to wait until 1957 when, as a 32-year old playing in the Third South with Southend, he scored Northern Ireland's first ever winner at Wembley on his only international appearance.

Since then the 1964 Cup semi-final team had an Irish accent, with the Republic's Noel Dwyer in goal and northerner Jimmy McLaughlin, goalscorer in the semi, up front. Scottish international Tommy Craig played his part in the ascent under Toshack.

The end of the 1980s saw a Scottish influx. Striker John Hughes from Berwick has enjoyed greater success as a manager, his record with Falkirk making him a popular candidate to succeed Roberto Martinez before Hibs stepped in. Striker Paul Chalmers proved too lightweight – a failing reproduced by a later Scottish Swan, the under 21 international Colin McDonald – and the best was the least apparently promising of the trio, Keith Walker. Signed like Chalmers from St Mirren, Walker's performances as a slow, rugged midfielder convinced

Scotsman Lachlan McPherson was a promotion winner in 1924–5.

SWANSEA TOWN F.C. - DIV.3 (S) CHAMPIONS 1949

LEFT TO RIGHT - BACK ROW :- KEANE, FEENEY, F.BARSON (Trainer), WESTON, PARRY, PAUL, W.McCANDLESS (Manager), BURNS.
FRONT ROW :- PAYNE, McCRORY, POWELL, SCRINE, MORRIS.

Irishmen Rory Keane, Jim Feeney and Sam McCrory emulated him in 1948–9

the astute Frank Burrows that he made the makings of a decent centre-half. 'Sky' Walker went on to form a highly successful partnership with Mark Harris and play for the rest of the nineties, making 270 league appearances.

Among recent players Lee Trundle proclaimed an ambition – as yet unrequited – to play for the Republic of Ireland, while current wing Tommy Butler has two caps and full-back Marcos Painter, a youth international, has every reason still to hope. Record signing Craig Beattie extended the Scottish connection late in August 2009.

Q is also for **Queen's Park Rangers.** Not always favourite opponents – the 3–0 League Cup defeat at Loftus Road in 2004 may be the worst single performance of recent years – but a frequent source of managerial talent. John Hollins and Kenny Jackett were both assistant managers at Loftus Road. Both took the Swans into League One, an achievement fans would prefer their latest Rangers refugee, Paulo Sousa, not to emulate.

R is for

Red Card, an object shown too often to Swans players, with a fresh peak of three in the league cup-tie against Scunthorpe in late August 2009. Reports suggested the usual mix of provocation, poor refereeing and indiscipline.

Traditions of the long, lonely walk date well before cards were invented. A much-quoted statistic in the 1970s was that the Swans had had more players sent off since the war than any other club, starting with Frankie Burns in the first postwar match. Jim Feeney and Jack O'Driscoll went following the epic goalmouth brawl against Reading at Christmas 1948. Disciplinary statistics under Harry Gregg suggested the team was carrying machetes, but goals-against showed they were not.

The costliest departure may have been Colin West's in the 1993 playoff at West Brom, although greater attention would have been paid to Marc

Richards' late-season dismissal at Hartlepool 10 years later if relegation had followed. Fastest sending-off was Walter Boyd, a substitute despatched before the game had restarted against Darlington at the Vetch. Prize for the daftest is shared by Barry Hole, raising his hand to the referee to show what a Port Vale player had done to him, and Tony Bird, throwing mud at a linesman at Cambridge.

With cards more frequent in the modern game, players have put together sequences of sendings-off. The inoffensive Kris O'Leary was undone by lack of pace and mistimed tackles while Richie Appleby's petulance contributed to seeing red in consecutive matches, and another a month later.

Teams with nine or ten men often raise their game, but the real price comes in suspensions. About the only happy moment the Swans had at Bristol Rovers' grimly inadequate Twerton Park was Michael Basham's last minute equaliser for a 9-man team in August 1995. The bill

Jim Feeney, dismissed after a memorable brawl

was paid eight months later, the slide to relegation begun by early-season suspensions.

Roger Freestone. So good they named him seven times – as in the North Bank chant of 'Roger. Roger, Roger. Roger, Roger. Roger, Roger Freestone!' Whatever else was wrong with Swans teams between 1991 and 2004 – and there was often plenty – compensation came in watching a goalkeeper the equal of any in the club's history. In an era of instability, decline and often outright fear, Roger Freestone provided continuity and assured quality. He was a goalkeeper in the modern idiom created by the abolition of the back-pass, not merely a brave shot-stopper and resolute interceptor of crosses,

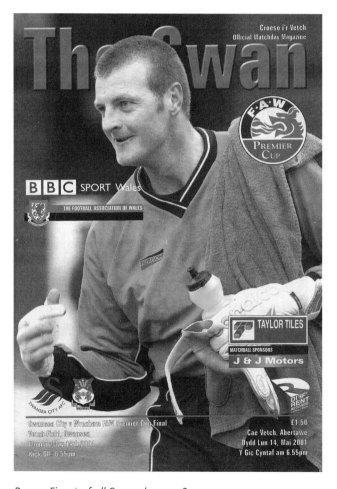

Roger: Finest of all Swans keepers?

but an additional sweeper who commanded his own penalty area and had sufficient footballing skill to cope beyond it. Uncoincidentally his best periods were when he played behind a stable centre-back pairing – Mark Harris and Keith Walker in the 90s then Matthew Bound and Jason Smith early in the new century – with the instinctive, anticipatory mutual understanding that is the foundation of solid defence. They certainly knew about Roger, vocal to the extent that his voice would dwindle to a hoarse late-season croak. Off the field they had to reckon with a sense of humour that, according to his biographers, majored in practical jokes involving clingfilm and toilet bowls.

One of the last Newport County league players active, Roger reached the Vetch via Chelsea, on loan in 1990 then permanently the year after, perhaps the best of many good deals made by Frank Burrows. He showed incredible consistency and durability over the next 13 seasons, his only lengthy absence in 2003 when loanee Neil Cutler played the final 13 matches of the cliffhanging battle against relegation to the Conference. The one drawback was that his deputies tended to rust through inactivity. Lee Jones played six league matches in four seasons before proving himself a decent keeper elsewhere, while successor and namesake Jason's 10 appearances in five years were marked by nervy accident-prone defensive efforts such as the seven goals conceded at Hartlepool and four that might have been seven at Rushden. Some of Roger's most memorable moments involved penalties, not only the shotstopping heroics that won the Autoglass final at Wembley in 1994, but a brief spell as designated marksman. Three in a row were put away, making him leading scorer for a disturbingly long time into the 1995–6 season, before a miss led to reconsideration of the experiment.

There was one Wales cap, against Brazil at the Millennium in 2000, and a serious run at the Swans all-time appearance record, held since the 1930s by Wilfred Milne, that ended only 20 matches short when he was released by Kenny Jackett at the end of the 2003–4 season. He was disappointed the decision was not announced until after the final match, denying him and fans the chance to say goodbye. Nobody wants to field players who are bitter, depressed or demob-happy, but Roger argued that he would have been professional enough to give his best. He was surely right. After never letting down the Swans in his 565 previous league appearances, he'd hardly have done so at the last.

R is also for **Rangel, Angel** the full-back with the rhyming name who has been by far the most successful of the permanent signings made from Spain by Roberto Martinez. Signed from Terrassa in the *Segunda B,* Spain's regionalised four-part third division, Rangel immediately showed all the best qualities of the Spanish footballer – comfort on the ball, composure and ability

Angel Rangel: Rhyme and rhythm

to distribute, along with defensive solidity – in a seamless transition to the British game from the start of the 2007–8 season. He played 83 league games in his first two seasons, with hardly a bad one among them, providing the width and ability to play from the back essential to the current style.

And for **Real Madrid.** Spanish club who also play in all white, were beaten 3–0 on the Swans' summer tour in 1927 and have not troubled us since. The same cannot be said of **Rochdale,** venue for two of the most stressful afternoons in club history. On 26th April 1975 Spotland saw the stripping away of one of our few remaining distinctions – never having applied for re-election – when a 1–0 defeat left the Swans 22nd in the Fourth Division. Twenty-eight years to the day later, with something still worse threatened, the Swans played their final away match of the season there. A 2–1 victory helped preserve league status the following week. Those who were there still argue whether their experience was more agonising than others compelled to rely on the radio in a final 15 minutes when a hysterical BBC Wales commentary suggested Rochdale were about to score every time they crossed halfway.

S is for

Scotland, Jason. Less noticeable under Roberto Martinez than the Spanish armada, but arguably more influential, was the Trinidadian trio. Stocky, combative full-back Kevin Austin and Snoop Doggy Dogg lookalike centre-half Dennis Lawrence were joined in 2007–8 by striker Jason Scotland. Though never universally appreciated by Swans fans, many mistaking a languid

Medallion Man: Jason celebrates the League One title in 2008 RR

manner for laziness, he was one of the most formidable goalscorers and greatest bargains in the club's history.

Scotland cost £25,000 from St Johnstone and departed two years later for 80 times as much when he followed Martinez to Wigan. That rocketing value reflected two seasons in which he scored 45 league goals, just under a third of the Swans total, and was chosen by his fellow professionals for the PFA's League One and Championship XIs. Scotland has his limitations – if he didn't he would hardly have cost £25,000 or joined a League One club. He is not brilliant in the air and his first touch is variable. The role of solo striker in Martinez's preferred tactical scheme could leave him isolated and outnumbered.

These, though, were far outweighed by the ability to turn sharply and, with minimal backlift, fire hard, low shots with either foot that left the opposing keeper little time to react. Goals like this in both FA Cup ties against Fulham raised his profile and transfer value, as did the magnificent through ball that set up Nathan Dyer's goal in the earlier win at Portsmouth. Best of the lot, perhaps, came a season earlier when a ferociously swerving effort from well outside the penalty box salvaged a psychologically vital late point from a two-goal deficit against Bristol Rovers at the Liberty Stadium. At 30 his desire for a Premiership chance was understandable, and £2m for a striker of his age seemed reasonable compensation. Replacing his goals was an early challenge facing Paulo Sousa.

Supporter. Players and managers come and go, often at minimal notice. Fans, though, are lifers, prisoners of an allegiance that allows no early release for good behaviour.

Supporting the Swans has rarely been a glamorous choice, default option of the unimaginative in the way proclaimed affection for Manchester United, Arsenal or Chelsea so often is. For most it expresses a deeper allegiance, formed through ancestry, childhood or residence, to South-West Wales and a city which as historian Glanmor Williams wrote: "has a history unsurpassed in length, importance, variety and interest" among Wales's major settlements.

They are not necessarily more passionate than other fans – passion is felt for all clubs – but perhaps more noisily expressive of it. There is a self-consciousness Welshness which differentiates them from 22 of 23 league opponents. While never likely to be mistaken for a Cymanfa Ganu, Swans fans are more tuneful than the league norm, the massed chorus of *'Falling in Love With You'* at Newcastle in 1995 surprising a Spurs-supporting friend genuinely impressed by what we all took for granted.

West Walian wit – verbal and relishing the ludicrous – also has its moments. Derby County's Rammy the Ram was greeted at Pride Park by a joyful chorus

At the Millennium 2006.   RR

of 'sheepshagger', the anti-Welsh pejorative of choice of the dimmer English fan, while a sudden police influx at Rotherham inspired a chant of 'It's Just Like Watching The Bill'.

They can also embarrass. Football architecture expert Simon Inglis reckoned Elm Park the dullest ground in England, but that was no reason to try to demolish it in 1993. Kneejerk anti-English and anti-Cardiff chanting matter less than sporadic violence and racism, but are no less tediously irritating.

The local *Sporting News* spotted an archetype as early as 1921: "Generally he is short of stature, anaemic looking, with a head too big to suggest it contains only brains, a high shrieking voice, reminiscent of a rusty saw in a quick staccato action. He is blind to every move to initiated by the Swansea Town players, but his attention to a faulty clearance or badly placed pass is microscopic". He is still with us, although better fed and computer-literate, the internet message board a fresh outlet for his discontents.

The main criticism of Swans fans, though, is that there are rarely enough of them. Brian Tabner's research shows a club that attracted support better than average in its own division in the early to mid 1920s, but since likelier to

So close you could touch it: Fans on the promotion trail at Plymouth, 1979

drop below the norm. A peak was attained, in line with League attendances as a whole, in 1948–9 when Vetch Field crowds averaging 22,535 saw the Swans win Division Three South. The low point was 1974–5, 89th best supported club in the league, averaging 2,070.

The modern fan is probably armed with a mobile phone, pre-assigned seat number and replica shirt rather than the cap, scarf and pack of cigarettes that characterised his predecessor on the North Bank in the 1950s. Websites have made him better informed about the club and its doings, and also supplied a means of networking and organisation that was hugely valuable in the battle to eject Tony Petty. The growth of the Supporters Trust has given him a stake and a say in the club which he sustains, an idea which terrified the Swans Board in the late 1940s.

He (and it is still mostly he) remains, though, essentially the same being – a local patriot with a taste for beer and wordplay, who wants most of all to see the Swans win, but also has the preference for open, stylish football that runs through the club's history and revived under Brian Flynn and Roberto Martinez. There are, and have been thousands of them, many now into third and fourth generations. One must stand for all – Terry Coles, personification of the innocent bystander, who went to see the already-promoted Swans play for the Third Division championship at Rotherham in 2000 and never returned home, the victim of a police horse.

Sykes, Joe. If he had done nothing other than spot the teen-aged Ivor Allchurch playing park football on the Cwm Level in 1944, Joe Sykes would be honoured in Swans history. He did much more. The first in the line of 'good and faithful servants' continued by Harry Griffiths and Alan Curtis, Sykes was an adopted rather than native Swan, but no less popular or significant for that. Nobody has matched him for sheer length and variety of service, arriving from Sheffield Wednesday in 1924 and only finally leaving when long past statutory retirement age in 1968. As a player he was captain and centre-half of the best Swans team pre-Toshack, Third Division South champions in 1924–5, FA Cup semi-finalists and fifth in Division Two the year after. Small for a centre-half at 5 ft 9 in, he more than compensated with positional sense, timing and cultured footballing gifts that meant no description was complete without reference to his mastery of the 'carpet pass'. Retiring after 313 league games in 1935, he returned briefly to Sheffield, but was back in Swansea during the war years and in 1947 was appointed assistant coach to Frank Barson, whom he succeeded in 1954.

OGDEN'S CIGARETTES.

J. SYKES.
SWANSEA TOWN.

Sheffield by birth, Swansea from a lifetime of service

His coaching emphasised the pure values of his own game. Cliff Jones reckoned him 'one of the shrewdest judges of ability I've known', recalling that he managed to be both 'respected and popular'. He became assistant manager under Trevor Morris in 1960 and caretaker manager six years later, aged nearly 69. Inheriting a team hopelessly bottom of Division Three, he arrested its headlong decline – although not sufficiently to avert relegation – before handing over to Billy Lucas in February 1967. He finally retired at the end of the following season.

S is also for **Schadenfreude** which sounds like an opponent on a pre-season tour of the Netherlands, but is really the art of taking pleasure in the misfortunes of others. Swans fans are good at it. If most deeply felt when something bad happens to Cardiff City, it also applies to the inability of Leeds United to extract themselves from League One. Aside from the fact that Swans fans love Leeds and chairman Ken Bates as much as followers of every other club, there is also the matter of Andy Robinson. An engagingly creative attacker who came late to league football, and whose creeping baldness and hunched-up figure strongly hint at how he will look in old age, he was perfectly entitled,

THE SWANSEA CITY ALPHABET

Andy Robinson contemplates a future at Elland Road   AT

after fulfilling his contract, to opt for the bigger money closer to home offered by Leeds in the summer of 2008. His reward has been consecutive playoff frustrations and the dubious pleasure of staring up the league at his former club. Wigan mishaps have recently acquired similar currency.

And for **Speedy.** Upwardly mobile centre-half Nigel Stevenson was the constant factor in the roller-coaster era that took the club from Fourth to First to Fourth. A solid defender who in his coltish early days suggested an animated anglepoise lamp, he proved more durable than the initially more promising

Learning from a Legend. An extremely youthful Nigel Stevenson (no 5 on shorts) and other apprentices listen to John Charles

Steve Morris. His spectacular goal against rivals Blackburn was vital to the promotion to the First he helped secure at Preston by playing on while injured. He won four Welsh caps and later played one of his finest matches at the Vetch…for Cardiff City.

And also **Sam Ricketts,** a full-back from an unusual background for a footballer – son of a famous showjumper Derek Ricketts – who has shown some ability to clear obstacles in his own career, surviving release from Oxford United and the collapse of Telford United. He was perhaps the best signing made by Kenny Jackett, extracted for nothing from the wreckage of Telford in 2004. Ricketts was a model of tidily unpretentious competence over two seasons in which he played 86 out of 92 league matches, sealing his wing against attackers and at the same time an effective contributor to the Swans own assaults. As well as the horsy folk, he has Welsh ancestry that has enabled a handy international career. Choosing to move on to Hull in 2006, he was an equally consistent presence in their rise to unprecedented Premier League status within two seasons. Sold to Bolton Wanderers in the summer of 2009, the transfer fee included sell-on money that came as a handy windfall for the Swans.

T is for

Gosh, it's Tosh

Toshack, John. Three decades on it still seems like a hallucination, rising in a little over four years from the Fourth Division to sixth place in the First. It was hard not to see manager John Toshack as some sort of alchemist, particularly since he also scored vital last-day goals against Halifax in 1978 and Chesterfield, a powerful header eight minutes from time, a year later. Even if you balance the ledger with the equally rapid return journey and the final reckoning in the High Court in late 1985, it is an extraordinary feat.

It was sometimes attributed rather too glibly to Liverpool connections and advice from mentor Bill Shankly. There's no doubt Toshack learnt plenty from one of the great British club sides, and a rare top-class manager who left a system that outlived him.

This, though understates the quality of his inheritance, a club revitalised and reinstructed in good footballing habits by Harry Griffiths, that had barely missed promotion the year before and had three youngsters of the highest quality in Alan Curtis, Robbie James and Jeremy Charles, plus two others later capable of playing in the First Division.

It also does insufficient credit to the self-sufficient intelligence and confidence of Toshack himself. These have enabled him to spend most of his subsequent career far from home, mostly in Spain, a footballing culture which prizes tactical sophistication above all else. Not the least of his achievements at Swansea was devising the prototype – involving a solo striker, sweeper and wing-backs – of the formation Spaniards still call the *sistema Toshack*. It enabled the dash and panache that took Division One unawares in 1981–2.

Before the fall: John Toshack and the team who took the Swans to sixth in the league, 1982

You also need to be pretty secure in your self and your place amid changing-room machismo to not only publish a volume of poetry, but give it a title – *Gosh It's Tosh* – that sounded dangerously like a review.

British football has produced few more cosmopolitan figures. Yet he remained unmistakeably Cardiffian, that 'A' sound evident even in his deliberate, precise Spanish. Though he became one of us by adoption, and so an object of some ambivalence to his native city, he is also the most significant player produced by Cardiff in the past half-century, their answer to Swansea's explosion of talent in the 1950s. His departure commanded as much space in Cardiff's centenary brochure as their excruciating title near-miss in 1924. It was suitable that he should score his final goal at Ninian Park, taking approximately seven and a half minutes to lumber from halfway on Boxing Day 1983 but with no doubt about the final outcome from the moment he took possession.

By then the miracle-worker label was up for review. The Swans were heading for a second consecutive relegation, the financial crash gathering with still greater pace and Toshack, who had fallen out very publicly with most of his senior players a year earlier, was working with a severely depleted squad. He had already walked out once, and the sack was not far away.

But that he has not managed a British club since has been solely his choice. His achievements over that extraordinary period between March 1978 and May 1982 remain both indelible and scarcely credible.

Trevor Ford

Trevor, an old-fashioned centre-forward with modern views of his own worth

Trevor Ford holds a place in Swansea mythology scarcely explained by an official record of nine goals in 16 matches before departing for Aston Villa in January 1947. Those records exclude the previous year when, with clubs from the top two Divisions divided into League North and League South, Ford burst from previous obscurity to become the most dangerous attacker in the country, scoring 40 goals and terrifying almost as many goalkeepers. He was still living with his parents on Townhill and awestruck schoolboys would vie for the honour of sitting next to him on the bus home.

The forerunner of the Swans extraordinary postwar explosion of home-grown talent, he had been a full-back and the youngest ever Swansea Schools player in 1938, but converted into a forward during war service. He was in every way an assertive player – a centre-forward in the traditional hardshooting, keeper-charging mould – and a tough negotiatior who, when most players were restricted by deference and the maximum wage, knew his own worth and battled to get it.

His style on the field was spectacularly encapsulated in the final half-hour of his debut for Sunderland in 1952. He broke his marker's jaw, scored a hat-trick and snapped a goalpost. But he resented suggestions that he deliberately harmed goalkeepers, suing England keeper Gil Merrick for allegations in his autobiography.

That typified his off-field combativeness. He left the Vetch after an argument about preparations for an FA Cup tie and his revelations about under-the-counter payments at Sunderland helped end not only his own career in British football, but the maximum wage.

Trevor described himself as a businessman and his autobiography *I Lead The Attack* is as much about money as football, but he was good enough to score 23 goals in 38 games for Wales and be voted one of the 100 Football League legends in 1998.

He later worked, suitably for his name, in the motor trade and was proud of the upward social mobility that saw his sons privately educated and a grandson at Eton. His son Martyn has been a Conservative council candidate in Swansea, not the family's only connection with the party. *I Lead The Attack* was ghosted by Cardiff sportswriter Howard Green, father of current MP and front-bench spokesman Damian. Trevor died in 2003.

T is also for **Tate, Alan,** longest-serving of the current first team regulars. A Geordie who came from Manchester United, initially on loan as one of the saviours of 2003, he is a centre-half with the footballing skills needed for a variety of positions. Sometimes used as a midfielder, he spent much of the 2008–9 season filling in for the injured Marcos Painter at full-back and even played 75 calm, trouble-free minutes in goal against QPR after Dorus de Vries was hurt. Lapses of concentration have sometimes compromised undoubted talents.

Fit for many purposes: Alan Tate AT

And for **Throw, Long,** speciality of Andy Legg, a lively winger who came to the Swans as a 22 year old in 1988 via Briton Ferry in the Welsh League. Legg's throws amazed not merely through their length – he could reach the far post from the touchline and bombard the penalty spot from halfway – but for the apparent ease with which such power was generated by a smallish frame. After 162 games for the Swans he played more than 400 for other clubs including Cardiff before cancer forced his retirement when nearly 40. His book *Alive and Kicking* chronicles both his career and his battle with the illness.

And also **Trust, Supporters.** Along with the move from the Vetch to the Liberty, the club's most important development of the 21st century. The Supporters Trust movement grew out of the greater fan activism – represented by fanzines and the Football Supporters Association – of the late 1980s and 1990s. For decades fans had been asking for a say in their clubs, and invariably been ignored. In 1947 the Swans Board was terrified by the mere idea that the Supporters Club might put up nominations. Eventually came recognition that they had to get organised and use their combined purchasing power to buy their way in as sharehold-ers. Pioneered at Northampton in the early 1990s, the idea was given real momentum by government funding for an umbrella organisation, Supporters Direct, from 2000.

Supporters Trust membership card – 2007–08 season

For the Swans, as with many clubs, it took a crisis to make it happen. The late Richard Lillicrap advocated a trust from early 2000 but the real push came a year later with realisation that current owners Ninth Floor had had enough, and there was no plausible owner in sight.

Formed in the summer of 2001 and formally launched in the Patti Pavilion on 27th August, the Trust arrived with perfect timing for the battle against Tony Petty, who took control in October. It brought something else new – a conversation with a Supporters Direct staffer that autumn was the first time I can remember hearing the words 'Swansea City' and 'well organised' in the same sentence.

Its role in that battle, including one 2,000 strong pre-match demonstra-tion, meant it had an unanswerable claim to board representation as part of the Mel Nurse-led consortium when it finally ousted Petty in January 2002.

Payment of an annual £10 subscription gives fans membership and the right to vote in elections for a committee currently chaired by Phil Sumbler which in turn nominates a director, currently Huw Cooze. The Trust's 18 per cent shareholding, plus democratic credibility, gives him a voice to be reckoned with in Board deliberations.

U is for

Ugly, Lovely Town, Dylan Thomas's famous evocation of Swansea's undoubted quirkiness. The city's most famous literary figure had little to do with the Swans, certainly nothing remotely approaching his fellow-poet Dannie Abse's lifelong passion for Cardiff City. A joyous essay of Abse's explains how he went on poetry reading tours with Laurie Lee, who had a girl in every town while Danny had only his Cardiff City fixture list. He also describes whiling away sleepless nights by summoning up images of players: "All wear the Bluebird shirt. Some announce their famous names; Trevor Ford, John Charles, Mel Charles, Ivor Allchurch, all of whom played for Cardiff in their declining football years". No Swans fan can read that sentence without remarking that all four came from Swansea.

Dylan's sole reference appears to be in his short story 'The Fight' in which he and a new friend 'sat on a sofa in the window and talked as though we had always known each other. Would the 'Swans' beat the 'Spurs?'. No answer is given, although results around the time when he was 15 and threequarters – the age given in the story – suggest it was probably 'No'. Although Stephen Knight, the 'Sandfields Baudelaire' has channelled Swansea demotic into his poem 'At the Foot of Division Four' including the couplet

Ivor invades Dannie Abse's subconscious wearing the wrong shirt

John Toshack wozzermarr-Nidjer wenn
A roe-zupp 2 Division won

this round probably goes to the old enemy, even if they borrow our players to do it with.

Elsewhere in literature Ernest Gann's *Soldier of Fortune* (1954) tells of Inspector

Merryweather of the Hong Kong Police: "The tragic news had come across the London wireless just before Merryweather departed for patrol and he had not had a chance to discuss the disaster with anyone. And so he brooded, for Merryweather came from Swansea where the nights were cool instead of wretchedly humid. Yes, back in Swansea there would be a good many chaps willing to explain how West Ham notched up a score of four while Swansea managed only one". Idioms and means of transmission have changed since then, but we still all know how he felt.

Nor might Dylan Thomas have wished to acknowledge kinship with Roger Evans' *Swansea City* song of 1978, in particular the immortal couplet 'Therefore for the replay, we went to White Hart Lane'. But Evans supplied not only an answer to Dylan's Swans v Spurs question, 'You should have heard the cockerel cry, when the Swans scored number three', but a terrace anthem unique to the Swans that is still sung more than 30 years on.

Most vivid perhaps of all Swans connections to the arts is the film *Twin Town* (1997) in which the twins played by Rhys and Llŷr Ifans not only debate the difference in shape between corner flags at the Vetch and Ninian Park, but commit a brutal premeditated murder while wearing 95–6 vintage shirts, about the most interesting thing anyone did in that particular strip.

U is also for **Unfavourite.** In theory every Swans player is to be cherished. In practice there are some we never like. Most of us have an unfavourite player. Many speak harshly of Charlie Hartfield. Some even fail to love Kris O'Leary. The personal choice is Andy Gurney, a Kenny Jackett acquisition. We've had worse players, but none less prepossessing. He had a shaven head, a strange lurching run and proved that tough guys can be weak defenders and tall men can be poor in the air. When he was sent off at Kidderminster, we missed him so badly that we won 5–1. One attempted tackle at Scunthorpe may have been the worst challenge seen in 43 years watching the Swans.

And for **Unlisted**, but not forgotten.Limited space regrettably prevents further mention of:

Bowen, Jason Diminutive, direct, pacy attacker who sparkled in 1993 play-off chase. Wasted on Birmingham, prospered at Cardiff.

Ian Callaghan, both gentleman and player, with scarcely a foot or pass out of place.

Jonathan Coates, gifted lightweight midfielder, rated by Jan Molby for his vision and unselfishness.

Geoff Crudgington, athletic keeper signed after stopping Alan Curtis one on one for Crewe.

Glen Davies, 145 league appearances, most by any of our many Davieses.

Gordon Davies, only pre and post Second World War league player.

Christian Edwards. Gifted local 90s centre-back, never quite fulfilled great talent.

Adrian Forbes, hardworking wide midfielder, scorer of last league goal at the Vetch.

David Giles. Kevin Keegan lookalike, played for all four Welsh clubs, a Cardiffian who scored a memorable late winner against them in the New Year's Day 1980 derby.

Mark Gower, wide man whose ability to hit posts and crossbars without ever scoring remains a source of wonder.

Besian Idrizaj, anyone for Scrabble?

Izzy Iriekpen cool, classy centre-back, occasionally too cool for comfort.

Steve Jenkins, local boy made Welsh international full-back in the nineties.

Lenny Johnrose, muscular midfield complement to Martinez, goal helped prevent relegation in 2003

Pat Lally, tidy, hirsute 70s midfielder, later a Players Union official.

Billy Lucas, wing adept at winning freekicks by tying his own legs into knots, later manager as well.

John Mahoney, Tosh's cousin, tough driving midfielder whose broken leg was crucial to relegation in 1983.

Andy McFarlane, scorer of two immortal goals, at Wembley against Huddersfield and in a Vetch playoff for West Brom (too bad he was still playing for us).

David Morris, not as Welsh as he sounds, but much more interesting, an East End Jew who, after 215 goals for Swindon and five for us, wound up in California.

Glen Davies

Billy Lucas

Tony Millington goes to ground against England watched by Mel Nurse (rear, dark shirt)

Tony Millington, proof that goalkeepers really are crazy.

Aidan Newhouse. If he'd been Spanish he'd have been called Casanova, and still wouldn't have scored.

Colin Pascoe, gifted, ultimately unfulfilled, winger turned coaching staff stalwart.

Clive Slattery would get you nowhere, but nor would Zico in some of the teams he played for.

Carl Slee, master of the mistimed tackle.

Jason Smith quick, adept centre-half before an injury that ended his career, and arguably John Hollins's.

James Thomas whose greatest day, the status-preserving hat-trick against Hull, was one of his last free from injury.

Max Thompson, scored perhaps the greatest Vetch goal, a volley against Arsenal, followed by an ecstatic dash that had spectators in the East Enclosure wondering if he'd stop in time.

Chris Todd, beat cancer, back in the league with Exeter.

Steve Torpey, target-man, good in the air, with an excellent first touch…and a dreadful second one.

V is for

Vetch Field, of blessed memory. A dump, but our dump. The first, and only, ground the Swans had for 93 years, from foundation in 1912 to the move to the Liberty Stadium in 2005. Not always a field of dreams, but certainly one of vivid memories, good and bad, collective and individual.

There are seaside grounds like Bloomfield Road and Deportivo La Coruna's Estadio Riazor. There are city centre stadiums like St James's Park, Newcastle and Molyneux. Few combine the two like the Vetch, a couple of blocks from the sea front and scarcely further from Oxford Street and the Quadrant shopping centre.

It was built on land leased from the Swansea Gaslight company, the first spectator accommodation spoilheaps of ash and brick offering views of a

As it was, with the North Bank (left) in its untamed pre-1951 incarnation

VETCH FIELD—SWANSEA CITY F.C.
BY TED FOXTON

As it became, with the North Bank (right) roofed and the Double Decker still the defining structure

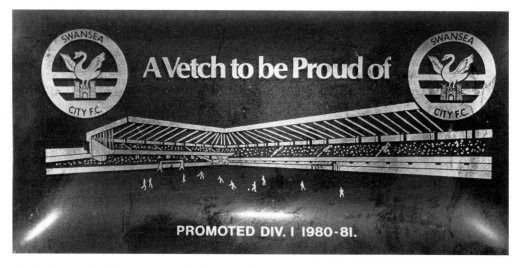

Best Laid Plans. Early 80s visions, of which only the East Stand happened   RR

cinder pitch on which players had to wear kneepads. Turf, and more sophisti-
cated viewing positions arrived in 1913 but the Vetch never quite threw off
that industrial ruggedness. Its development was always cramped by its sur-
roundings, with terraced streets, the prison, the Drill Hall and until 1925 the
Vetch Field Junior School setting the limits.

To some it became 'the old lady', but it was always vigorously, raucously
masculine, a cockpit whose confined spaces and raw acoustics spooked many
visiting teams. When several London clubs who thought themselves better

Stadium of light. Seen from Townhill during the final season   AT

fell at the Vetch in 1945–6, Charlton manager Jimmy Seed recorded: "The
Vetch Field is a very compact ground. The playing pitch is smaller, which
allows no room for working and the crowd seems to be on top of the players,
giving a cramping atmosphere."

If the Liberty Stadium has the uniformity of a single architectural vision
made concrete and metal, the Vetch's structures were a potted club history,
each the product of a period of relative prosperity. The upward mobility of
the 1920s accounted for the North Bank, constructed in 1925 and the West
Stand, described by Percy Young in 1954 as 'the crazy two-tiered stand behind

At the end. Fans gather in front of the Centre Stand following the final league match against Shrewsbury, 2005 RR

one goal', popularly known as the Double-Decker and offering one of the best views in football.

The 1950s accounted for the upgrading of the North Bank, its roof and the floodlights, while the grandstand that loomed over the East End for the Vetch's last quarter-century was the creation of the Toshack years. Opened in 1980 it was the first stage of a transformed 'Vetch to the proud of'. Like most football projects of the period it did not progress, leaving the new stand exposed to the elements and by the 1990s, like the club, somewhat the worse for wear.

Below it was the levelled-off remnant of the old, formerly railway-sleepered Small Bank. My father, back from national service in 1949 and one of the last people allowed to climb the back of the bank for a match against Leyton Orient, recalls: "Every time we scored, the crowd moved, and I was knocked back down to the bottom".

The Bradford fire did for the wooden Double Decker, object of attempted arson by Leeds fans in 1981 and replaced by a simple canopy over the standing enclosure. Other safety measures systematically eroded capacity until the ground closed with its capacity around a third of the 32,796 who saw Arsenal play an FA Cup tie in 1968.

As it now is, from the outside. Pic: Huw Richards

Yet it retained the noisy, demotic ambience that helps account for disparities between the Swans' home and away form. In 1948–9 a draw with Southend prevented only the second 100 per cent home record in league history, while results at the Vetch were the difference between relegation and survival in five of the following 14 seasons. Among the 128 teams who played league football between 1888 and 2002, the Swans rank 38th on home record, 89th away. The final Vetch tally was 908 league wins, 420 defeats and 380 draws, goals for 3048, against 1821.

As it now is, reverting to nature   AT

Rugby League, with some memorable Wales matches, boxing featuring such ring masters as Brian Curvis, Howard Winstone and Ronnie James and music varying from Stevie Wonder to one-hit wonder Carl Douglas – his concert a financial disaster rather than the money-spinner the Board had hoped – also graced the Vetch.

Catering and toilets were famously bad, and exposed as such in national surveys, but the old ground ended well. The last league season, 2004–5, was the first in which it hosted the highest gates in a division. The last league match, a victory over Shrewsbury, paved the way for promotion a week later.

The impact of closure can be seen in the shuttering and boarding of the Garibaldi and the Clarence, the closest pubs. Four years on the Vetch is a rusting, overgrown hulk long overdue decent burial. Those 93 years of memories deserve better.

V is also for **Victims of Decline**, gifted players born at the wrong time who chose to stay through bad times, possibly sacrificing their careers. If the prototype is Herbie Williams, the description equally applies to 1960s midfielder Geoff Thomas and 1980s centre-back Dudley Lewis. Geoff was a gifted ballplayer and fierce striker of the ball who wound up as captain and sweeper in the 1974–5 re-election team. Dudley was a sweeper from the beginning, trusted at 18 with the role by John Toshack during the promotion run-in in 1981 and capped against Brazil two years later, after playing superbly as the Swans were relegated from the First Division. Each had a contemporary who left – for Herbie read Barrie Jones, for Geoff, John Roberts, for Dudley, Dean Saunders. The migrants won 111 caps, the stayers four. Maybe those who

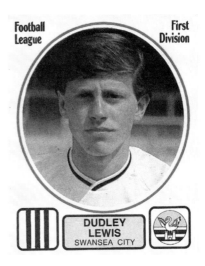

Dudley Lewis

left were simply better players, but they did not look it at the time. Perhaps leaving was evidence of – for Jones and Roberts at least, since Saunders was released and had no option – a greater determination that helped them to succeed. The stayers played a combined 1,097 league matches for the Swans, but must sometimes have wondered what might have been had they taken opportunities to leave. Loyalty clearly has its price, although the example of Stuart Roberts – a lively winger forced out as Tony Petty looked for sales, then disillusioned by the Wimbledon-blunted sensibilities of Wycombe boss Lawrie Sanchez – shows it can also be fatal to leave.

And also **Vic Gomersall,** a barrel-chested overlapping full-back from Manchester City who came to the Vetch in 1967 and proved one of the best, most durable acquisitions of a tough period, playing 180 matches over the next six years. Like many other immigrants he became an adopted South Walian, a highly effective commercial manager of Llanelli FC and for many years president of the Swansea Junior League.

W is for

White Rock, location and earlier name for the Liberty Stadium before it acquired its sponsored label, a glance at the city's industrial and sporting past as home of the White Rock Copper Works where the James brothers – Swansea rugby heroes of the 1890s – were labourers.

The project was first mentioned in the *Evening Post* in 1985 and discussed so long that most fans progressed beyond cynical to satirical, but came to pass in 2005 as an enterprise shared between the Swans, the Ospreys and Swansea City Council. Two venerable city-centre sites, both council-owned, were swapped for a purpose-built, joint-use 20,500 capacity – at least for rugby, which needs no cordon sanitaire between rival fans – stadium close to its edge. Much was lost – the Vetch's unique ambience and convenient location, plus

Liberty Stadium, photographed from Mayhill.   RR

more than 90 years of shared memory. The Builders Arms gave way to various Hafod and Plasmarl hostelries plus Rossi's chippie. The North Bank, deprived of the option of standing, has attempted to reconstitute itself in the East Stand.

The pluses involve more head than heart – vastly improved toilets, refreshment facilities and a pitch that has withstood the rigours of groundsharing to deliver surfaces ideally suited to the stylish football played under Roberto Martinez. Functional rather than elegant – at least until breeze block interiors become fashionable – its capacity and comfort have given the Swans commercial potential undreamt of at the Vetch, although perhaps still insufficient for progress beyond the Championship. The Ivor Allchurch statue provides both identity and focal point, with the words 'see you by Ivor' entering many a pre-match arrangement.

Collective memory inevitably takes time to accumulate and will not remotely match the Vetch until there are fathers telling sons and daughters tales of how they watched Jason Scotland and Ferrie Boddie in their own childhood. Nor has it become the fortress some hoped – poor late-season performances briefly jeopardised the League One championship won in 2008. But visiting fans compliment its comfort and atmosphere, which can seem subdued to those who grew up with the Vetch, and nobody would remotely contemplate going back, even if it were realistically possible.

Wilfred Milne. The best known fact about Wilfred Milne is that between 1920 and 1937 he set the Swans all-time record for league appearances, 586. Next is that he played more than 500 before he scored. What deserves to be better known is the fee paid to his Tyneside junior club Walker Celtic, a fish tea worth 2s 9d (14p in modern money).

The non-scoring defender used to be common, with some players rarely crossing halfway. Milne played in the same team as Harry Hanford, who made 200 appearances without scoring. After the war came Rory Keane, scoreless in 164 matches and Reg Weston, who scored once in 227 games.

What distinguished Milne was the sheer length of his scoreless spell, from his debut in September 1920 until Easter Monday 1934. Then, taking the penalty awarded to the Swans in a vital relegation clash with Lincoln City, he scored with a shot described as 'well placed'. The Swans won 1–0. That he had recently made his 500th league appearance – this was his 501st – was marked by a picture in the *Post,* but the belated breaking of his duck was, in keeping with an age much less given to record-keeping, not remarked.

Once it had happened there was, comparatively, no stopping him. He scored six times in the next season and a half, including a penalty in the final, relegation-saving victory over Plymouth, twice against Norwich – the first his only goal other than a penalty, 'a magnificent drive' from some 35 yards that

SWANSEA TOWN F.C. 1924-25

LEFT TO RIGHT - BACK ROW :- McPHERSON, E.EDWARDS (Trainer), MORRIS, COLLINS, LANGFORD, DENOON, MILNE, EDWARDS, NICHOLAS. FRONT ROW :- J.BRADSHAW (Manager), HOLE, DEACON, SYKES, FOWLER, THOMPSON, B.OWEN (Director).

Marathon Man: Wilfred Milne (third from right, back row) was already a seasoned pro when photographed with the rest of the first promotion-winning team, but with three-quarters of his career still to come

'sent the ball flying past the lined-up Norwich players into the net' – and two more against Brentford.

Milne's more usual qualities were noted in a 1924 match report praising his 'first-time volleying and sure tackling, and his fine judgment in taking the ball' against QPR.

That long career had a strange conclusion, at Easter 1937. Both goalkeepers were injured so Milne, long the emergency deputy, played in goal at Leicester and Nottingham Forest. Leicester, that year's Division Two champions, attacked incessantly and won 22 corners, but could not beat Milne, who played brilliantly in a 0–0 draw. The sequel at Forest was disappointing as the 'very tired' Swans went down 6–1. The Leicester match was, though, marked by an *Evening Post* picture spread whose caption 'Magnificent Milne' speaks for an entire career.

Wyndham Evans. Wyndham was perhaps the unlikeliest of the five survivors of Fourth Division football who played in the First Division for the

On target, in his early days as a goal-scorer

Swans. He had few pretensions as a stylish footballer, but never let the Swans down and, called up at moments of crisis, played beyond his supposed limits. In 1981 John Toshack recalled him for the run-in to promotion from Division Two and saw a rocky defense suddenly solidify.

Wyndham was a full-back from Llanelli whose musculature was liable to persuade nervous opponents that he was an escaped Scarlets back row. He was defensive solidity personified and a powerful tackler, albeit occasionally exposed for pace by the quickest attackers – a sending off at Brentford in 1978 followed a series of late tackles (Wyndham might have retorted that he had got there as fast as he could) on the distinctly nippy Steve Phillips.

He had spent some time as a makeshift striker and was among the leading scorers, with seven goals, in the re-election season. After that he pretty much gave up goals, managing only three more – all in one season – in his remaining 240 matches spread over 10 seasons. What came in return was a more mature, relaxed style of play encouraged by

Football League — First Division
WYNDHAM EVANS
SWANSEA CITY

Ambition attained, a First Division player

Harry Griffiths as an alternative to the over-aggressive approach under Harry Gregg. Wyndham totalled 389 matches for his only league club before going on a free to Pembroke Borough in 1986. His nephew Stuart Roberts later brought a very different physique and style to the Vetch as a lively winger, while Wyndham went on to be player-manager at Llanelli, taking the job after Robbie James died

W is also for **Waddle, Alan** and **Watkin, Steve,** strikers of different generations and standing with the Vetch crowd, each with a memorable goal in his pre-history. Waddle's one goal for Liverpool was the last in an Everton derby for a few years, while Watkin scored in bottom of the league Wrexham's FA Cup defeat of Arsenal. Waddle was the unparalleled hero of the late 1970s crowd, who could never imagine having the unearthly talent of Alan Curtis but saw themselves in Waddle's evident limitations and willingness to chase each ball and harass every opponent. North Bank chants insisted 'there's only one Alan Waddle' – some opponents may have suspected there were at least three – while a banner at Swindon proclaimed that he 'laid on more balls than Fiona Richmond'. Watkin by contrast became something of a butt in a period when the real inadequacy was in midfield. A point-blank miss at Oxford United has entered folk memory, forgetting that the opportunity owed much to Watkin's astute build-up work. His ability to hold, turn and shoot in busy penalty boxes was vital to making the Third Division play-offs in 1999, when he scored 17 goals.

And for **Williams,** a common name for Swans players. If Herbie was the best, the fastest was **John Williams,** the Flying Postman, who arrived as a wing or striker from Midlands club Cradley Town together with full-back Jon Ford in 1990 and left memories like his Usain Bolt-like domination of a field of football's fastest sprinters at Wembley and the utter bemusement of a Brentford defender who believed he was safely shepherding a pass back to his keeper only to have Williams dash around him and finish from a narrow angle. He played 113 matches in three spells, not always with beneficial effects on playing style. Once out of ideas,

Ashley Williams AT

team-mates were wont to thump the ball in his general direction, hoping that he'd get there first. Latest in the line is centre-half **Ashley Williams**. Noting the surname and hearing of his form for Stockport, Wales boss John Toshack sent an emissary who found that he was indeed qualified, via a mother whose name contains no hints at Welshness. A back-spun through pass on one of his first appearances at the Liberty suggested he was far from the conventional lower-league stopper, while sudden reincarnation as a goal-scorer was hugely welcome in early 2009–10.

And also **West Bromwich Albion** Amiably idiosyncratic Midlands club whose distinguished history has, unusually, not generated a corresponding sense of entitlement. Swans and Albion don't meet that often – 2009–10 is only their 11th season in the same division – but when they do, plenty happens. Those 20 league meetings have produced 83 goals, with 16 conceded on the first three visits to the Hawthorns in the late 1920s. Nor are memories of the playoff at West Brom in 1993 too happy, but in between Albion's ground saw two remarkable comebacks. One of few happy days in 1982–3, the First Division season Swans fans talk less about, was the fightback from a 3–0 deficit to draw 3–3 at the Hawthorns, with goals from Leighton and Robbie James and Jeremy Charles. Nine years later the Swans were subsiding with little resistance to a 2–0 defeat when midfielder Steve Thornber, previous record one goal in 98 matches, came on as a sub. Thornber scored a hat-trick in 10 minutes and the Swans won 3–2. Record signing Craig Beattie, who joined from Albion in August 2009, must hope to be heir to that freescoring heritage.

And **Weston, Reg.** Commanding stopper centre-half of the immediate post-war years, straight man to the spikiness of Frank Burns and the cultured skills of Roy Paul in an exceptional half-back line. Weston was captain of the team that won the Third Division South championship in 1948–9, although his attempt to address the Vetch Field crowd after the final match was thwarted by the failure of the public address system, a fate revisited upon manager Kenny Jackett following the last league match of all in 2005. His Swans career was ended abruptly after 229 matches in six league seasons by a dispute over housing – Tom Kiley stepping seamlessly into his position, and role as father figure.

X is for

Xenophobia. Hearing chants of 'England's full of ****' succeeded by 'We Hate Cardiff', one might think that Swans fans dislike anybody from east of Bridgend. It would also be idle to deny that there has been racism – incidents like the persistent booing of Plymouth's Ronnie Mauge one unhappy afternoon at the Vetch, idiotic songs about admittedly profoundly irritating Cardiff owner Sam Hammam and some comments about Jason Scotland show otherwise.

This coexists, though, with a majority taste for the different and exotic. Most European visitors to the Vetch were warmly welcomed, a not especially beguiling Lokomotive Leipzig team applauded off after beating John Toshack's

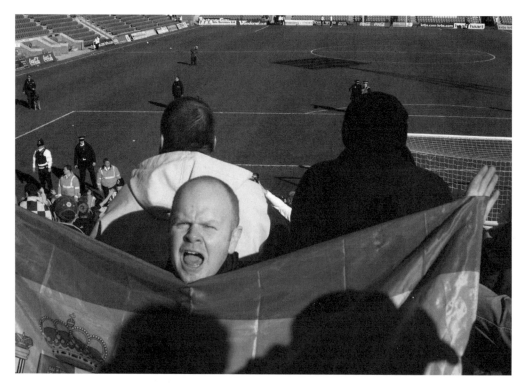

A Swans fan hails the Spanish armada   AT

title contenders in late 1981. Foreign players – a line beginning with two transients, the Hungarian John Haasz in 1960 and Dutch goalkeeper Nico Schroeder, the first player who qualified because Britain had joined the European Union, in 1976, who made one appearance apiece – have generally been warmly regarded.

One reason is that some – the brilliant Yugoslav duo of Dzemal Habziabdic and Ante Rajkovic in the Toshack years, contemporaries like Ferrie Bodde and Angel Rangel, or the angular Malian striker Mamade 'Big Mama' Sidibe, who has since found his level as a Premiership player with Stoke City – have been very good. Others, though, have been less successful and still liked. There was Joao Moreira, a full-back who had played as a junior for Benfica, who arrived during the Molby era – a decent footballer, but prone to lapses in concentration, who never quite adjusted to the British game. More was expected of Walter Boyd, a Jamaican striker who arrived in 1999 with a reputation for dazzling brilliance, insisted on wearing number 35 as a sign of his intention of breaking Cyril Pearce's single-season goalscoring record and looked capable of it after a two-goal debut, rounded off by a stunningly flighted chip, against Rotherham. You never quite knew what he would do next, he was always entertaining and the Swans did win the Third Division Championship, but the goal tally over two seasons fell rather short of Walter's predictions.

Recent seasons have seen Swans fans cheerfully brandishing Spanish flags, but even before that came a spell between 2000 and 2002 when French tricolors were the fashionable fan accessory in honour of persevering striker Matthias Verschave, lightweight midfielder David Romo and Nicolas Fabiano, a creator who looked to have serious long-term possibilities but has wound up in the French lower leagues with Paris Red Star. None lasted very long, but they could have few complaints about the warmth with which they were regarded. *Vive la différence*, as they say in St Thomas.

X is also for **eXile.** You may take the man (or woman) out of Swansea, but you rarely take Swansea out of them. Those who leave for work or family reasons are wont to take the Swans

Wish You Were Still Here: Richard Lillicrap   AT

with them, and transmit the addiction to successor generations. Exiles are particularly to be found on midweek winter nights at destinations a long way from Swansea, like Colchester and Carlisle, ensuring that the Swans still have their noisy, partisan following and enjoying the camaraderie of explorers in unfamiliar climes. One name must stand for many – the late Richard Lillicrap, son of a famous Swansea Borough Surveyor, pioneer advocate of a Swans Supporters Trust and board member of Supporters Direct, who died far too young in 2007 and is still much missed.

And for **X-ray.** Strains, pulls and broken bones are among the professional hazards of a sporting life, so footballers inevitably spend more time in the company of radiologists than most of us. Managers and fans can always tell you when an injured player is expected to return, with the implication that this will bring an upturn – forgetting the law of averages that says some-body else will be hurt in the meantime. Clubs simply have to live with them, although Paulo Sousa could have been forgiven for suspecting that Roberto Martinez's resignation letter had been accompanied by a gypsy curse as a succession of players went down in the early weeks of 2009–10.

Tom Kiley's knee remains the most famous injury in club history, but others have also been momentous. Two in particular may have sealed rele-

Lost leader: Colin Irwin

gation from Division One in 1982–3. It could be argued that any team that wins three promotions in four seasons must have enjoy a fair bit of luck. If so, it was repaid in full during 1982–3. First to go was club captain Colin Irwin, who after a solid first season was beginning to show the real authority that had won him rave reviews during his Liverpool apprenticeship and persuaded John Toshack to pay a club record £340,000. His knee went at Aston Villa in September. Still more damaging was the loss of rugged midfielder John Mahoney – John Toshack's cousin, and friend since childhood – whose influence, together with Bob Latchford's goals, was just about keeping the Swans afloat until he broke his angle on St David's Day, in the home defeat by Brighton. Perhaps relegation was inevitable – ending seven points from safety brooks little dispute. St David's Day, though, was when the slippery slope became a precipice, the drop likelier than not. Mahoney never played again, Irwin only four more times, their fate one that is feared every time a player suffers a serious, long-term injury. Ferrie Bodde, out for the rest of 2009–10 after snapping a cruciate for a second time, will need mental as well as physical strength to resume his career.

Y is for

Yorath, Terry who fills a distinct place in the Swans roll of oddity. Not only is he the only man to serve two separate spells – 'sentences' might be a fairer description – as manager, but appointment number two was made when the club was still taking legal action over the way the first term ended.

A tough and combative (opposing fans had other words) midfielder groomed in the Don Revie school at Leeds he led Wales in 42 of his 59 internationals and was warmly regarded by newspaper sub-editors with a taste for headlines like 'Alas, poor Yorath'. His first spell at the Vetch was the more successful as he helped reconstruct the club following the near-death experience of 1985–6, building a team that footballed its way out of the Fourth Division via the playoffs in 1988. This attracted the Football Association of Wales who needed a national manager and offered him the post part-time.

Yorath thought he could do it, but chairman Doug Sharpe whom he described as a 'bully' with a 'very hands-on approach' did not, exacerbating existing tensions. In 1989 Bradford City, a division higher and much closer to his Leeds home, offered Yorath their managership. He left with six months still on his contract, Sharpe sought an injunction and Yorath had to repay £18,000. He did not prosper at Bradford, nor did the Swans under his deputy Ian Evans. Less than a year later he was back. Spell two was an object lesson in never going back and after a club record nine consecutive defeats early in 1991 he was sacked. His memoirs, a confessional reflecting his Catholicism, record a tenure defined by 'money – or the lack of it'. Payment for player celebrations after promotion in 1988 came out of Yorath's own

Yorath in the red, as the Swans usually were when he was manager

pocket. Yet in spite of their differences, he had some affection for Sharpe 'the local builder made good – Sharpe by name and sharp by nature'

Y is also for **Yeovil,** league rookies turned unlikely mortal rivals who attracted the Liberty's largest football crowd, 19,288 for a league match in late 2005. Rising together in the 2004–6 period, rivalry between Wales and the West Country and Yeovil's Cardiff-born midfielder Gavin Williams celebrating a goal at the Vetch by performing the 'Ayatollah' in front of the North Bank all contributed to a genuine edge. The 2005 match saw one of Lee Trundle's most memorable goals in a 2–0 win. Yeovil were also the opponents when the Swans clinched the League One championship 2008, but it wasn't quite an unalloyed day of triumph. Yeovil won 2–1 to secure their own survival and the crown was clinched, amid crashing anticlimax, by results elsewhere.

Nigel Dalling at 17: already a league veteran

And for **Youthful Promise,** always cherished by Swans fans, particularly if local in origin. Like nobody else the local boy is an extension of ourselves and a harbinger of hope. The extreme is represented by Nigel Dalling, a small, neat winger who made his debut at 15 years and 289 days in 1974. For productivity there is nothing to equal the decade after the Second World War that produced Trevor Ford, the Allchurch and Charles brothers, Cliff Jones, Harry Griffiths and Terry Medwin. The greatest mystery is why a club that once produced such copious forward talent should more recently have specialised in defenders, with Chris Coleman and Andrew Melville the most distinguished Swans products since the mid 1980s, while fresh optimism attaches to teenagers like Jazz Richards and Kerry Morgan, given their chance by Paulo Sousa.

Z is for

dZemal hadZiabdic. To watch Jordi Gomez at the start of the 2008–9 season was to be reminded of the first sight of full-back Dzemal Hadziadbic in Swans colours in 1980, and the realisation that here was a player of a quality we had not signed in ages. When he made his competitive debut in a League Cup tie at Highbury, his name was known and he had played for Yugoslavia in a memorably brutal European Championship quarter-final at Ninian Park four years earlier, but this long before instant video updates on new signings from You Tube and websites.

An hour or so watching his speed and dexterity bemuse a far from clueless Arsenal team left little doubt of his class, or of the implication both that John Toshack was serious about taking the Swans into the First Division and that the board was prepared to back him. He was also, unlike the loanee Gomez, our player, signed from Velez Mostar.

The North Bank took one look at that name and rechristened him 'Jimmy', catching something of his cheerful good nature. He added a vital attacking dimension that helped drive that year's successful promotion campaign, giving width and pace to attacks and forming a lethally effective left-wing partnership with Leighton James. Jimmy appeared to relish London opposition – the Highbury debut followed a friendly appearance against Spurs, he scored a brilliant late-season goal against Chelsea and one of the highlights of the first First Division season was the unstoppable volley struck at home to Arsenal by Max Thompson from a free-kick Jimmy had floated ingeniously from the outside of his foot. By then he had been joined by a second, equally brilliant member of Yugoslavia's vast footballing diaspora, the sweeper Ante Rajkovic.

In all he played 89 league matches in three seasons, the last followed by a stand-up row with manager Toshack. He returned the best part of a decade later as a refugee from the civil war at home. The club played a benefit match for him and his family and he briefly

Jimmy

joined Alan Curtis on the development staff. He later became national coach of Qatar, taking it close to the 1998 World Cup finals before losing to eventual qualifiers Saudi Arabia.

Z is also for **Zeta-Jones, Catherine.** Actress from Swansea – origins evident in the film *Traffic*, where her accent oscillates uneasily between L.A and Mumbles – periodically rumoured to be buying in to the Swans. There is no evidence that she has any interest in football and rumour never shows the slightest sign of becoming reality, but the *Evening Post* and *Western Mail* are never likely to pass up the opportunity to print a picture.

And for **Zulu.** Film commemorating one of the better Welsh away performances – the 1879 defence by the South Wales Borderers of the Rorke's Drift Mission Station in what is now Kwazulu Natal, South Africa (also scene in 1995 of a less distinguished Welsh performance, the one serious car crash of my life). The refurbished Drill Hall next to the Vetch Field is named in honour of John Chard, who commanded the defence. That juxtaposition not infrequently comes to mind on away trips watching makeshift defences in danger of being overrun by rampant opponents, resistance stiffened by singing – some of it undoubtedly alcohol-fuelled – from travelling fans.

Outcomes over the years, it must be admitted, have been likelier to resemble Ishandlwana, the massacre of an entire British army that preceded Rorke's Drift, while hosts have rarely greeted Swans victories with the grace of the Zulu warriors shown acclaiming the defenders at the end of *Zulu*. Victory at Boston in 2005, from a penalty obtained via one of Lee Trundle's more artistically impressive stumbles, led to a rapid post-match education in the vehemence, variety and inventiveness of Lincolnshire invective. Not least of the joys of promotion in 2008 was winning at places previously associated with pain, frustration and defeat – Port Vale, Gillingham, Huddersfield, Yeovil and, most of all, Bristol Rovers. Years like that are, unavoidably, the exception. Following the Swans to away games is more usually summed up by those words of Brian Matthews' 'struggle, defeat and hope springing eternal'. It is also, though to travel in the company with others who share both a passion for a club whose condition is often serious, but rarely dull, and the memories and dreams that go with that passion. A triumph of hope over experience maybe, but a journey none of us would wish to miss.

BIBLIOGRAPHY

Alan Curtis Testimonial Souvenir Brochure – 2005
Bentley, Roy and Drury, Jim – Roy Wonder – Tempus 2005
Burgum, John – Swansea City AFC – Archive 1988
Charles, John – King of Soccer – Stanley Paul 1957
Charles, Mel – In the Shadow of a Giant – John Blake 2009
Cottey, Tony and Brayley, David – There's Only 2 Tony Cotteys – Gomer 2008
Davies, Dai – Never Say Dai – Siop y Siswrn 1986
Davies, James A (ed) – A Swansea Anthology – Seren 1996
End of an Era: The Vetch 1912–2005 Souvenir Brochure 2005
Farewell to the Vetch 1912–2005 – Evening Post 2005
Farmer, David – Swansea City 1912–82 – Pelham Books 1982
Farmer, David (with contributions from Jones, Colin and Lile, Brian) – The Swans, Town and City – Evening Post 2000
Farmer, David and Stead Peter – Ivor Allchurch M.B.E – Christopher Davies 1998
Foot, David – Beyond Bat and Ball – Aurum 1995
Ford, Trevor – I Lead The Attack – Stanley Paul 1957
Hayes, Dean – Swansea City Football Club An A-Z – Aureus 1999
Haynes, Keith and Sumbler, Phil – Vetch Field Voices – Tempus 2000
Hignell, Andrew – The History of Glamorgan County Cricket Club – Helm 1988
Hill, Jim – Swansea City AFC Official Annual 1980 – Christopher Davies 1979
Jenkins, John M, Pierce, Duncan and Auty, Timothy – Who's Who of Welsh International Rugby Players – Bridge Books 1991
Johnes, Martin – A History of Sport in Wales – University of Wales Press 2005
Jones, Cliff – Forward With Spurs – Stanley Paul 1962
Jones, Colin – Swansea Town/City AFC: The First Comprehensive Player A-Y – Cyhoeddwyr Dinefwr 2005
Laschke, Ian – Rothman's Book of Football League Records 1888–9 to 1978–9 – Queen Anne Press 1980
Legg, Andy – Alive and Kicking – Accent Press 2009
Murphy, Jimmy – Matt, United and Me – Souvenir Press 1968
Paul, Roy – A Red Dragon of Wales – Robert Hale 1956
Phillips, Gareth – Fan's Eye City: Swansea City in the age of the Premiership – London League Publications 2005
Risoli, Mario – Arrivederci Swansea, The Giorgio Chinaglia Story – Mainstream 2000

Roger Freestone Testimonial Brochure – 2001
Rothman's and Sky Sports Football Yearbooks
scfc.co.uk
Seddon, Peter J – A Football Compendium – British Library 1995
Shaw, Phil – The Book of Football Quotations – Ted Smart 2003
Shepherd, Richard – Swansea Town Football Club 1912–64 – Tempus 1988
Soccerbase.com
South Wales Evening Post (called the Daily Post until 1932)
Stead, Peter and Richards, Huw (eds) – For Club and Country: Welsh Football
    Greats – University of Wales Press 2000
Swansea City AFC Division One Official Souvenir – Evening Post 1981
Swansea Schools FA 75th Anniversary Book – Christopher Davies 1989
Tabner, Brian – Through The Turnstiles – Yore Publications 1992
Thomas, Dylan – Portrait of the Artist as a Young Dog – Dent 1940
The Vetch Field: A People's History – 2005
Yorath, Terry with Lloyd, Grahame – Hard Man, Hard Knocks – Celluloid 2004
Young, Percy – Football Year – Sportsman's Book Club 1958

Andrew Thomas's excellent photos of the Swans, and other Swansea themes can be found at pbase.com/andrew_thomas

INDEX

(Bold type to indicate main entries)